BEING GOOD AND DOING GOOD

By Martin E. Marty

Allan Hart Jahsmann, Editor

Fortress Press, Philadelphia

LEAD Books

LEAD Books are prepared under the direction of the Division for Parish Services, the Lutheran Church in America.

Designed and illustrated by Terry O'Brien.

Library of Congress Cataloging in Publication Data

Marty, Martin E., 1928–
  Being good and doing good.

  (Lead books)
  1. Christian ethics—Lutheran authors. I. Jahsmann,
Allan Hart. II. Title. III. Series.
BJ1251.M37 1984   241'.0404   84–47929
ISBN 0–8006–1603–0 (pbk.)

971F84   Printed in the U.S.A.   1–1603

CONTENTS

FOREWORD

Martin Marty has done the church a very important and valuable service in writing a book on Christian ethics, the nature and place of morality in the Christian life and the nurturing of it. The book will help Christians to avoid reducing the gospel and Christian faith to the law of love and other biblical directives. It also serves to counteract a sentimental, shallow teaching of the gospel apart from a dynamic relationship with God, a relationship in which God reigns through faith in Jesus Christ and obedience to him.

After reviewing various efforts at teaching virtue and moral behavior, Dr. Marty asks how we Christians are going to pass on and nurture moral values. His basic, pervading thesis is that "being good," which biblically means being declared and seen as good by God, liberates one for subsequent good actions so that "doing good" flows from "being good."

In the last two chapters the author also looks directly at the matter of Christian moral living in both private and public spheres of life. Addressing the connection between justification and sanctification in terms of practical life issues, the book shows how the Christian gospel gives people the power to do good without their making a claim on God or an idol out of their goodness.

This book is one of a series of small volumes called LEAD Books. These books are basic background readings designed primarily for lay leadership and teacher education in the church. A group study guide is available for leaders of a class course based on any of the texts. The study of *Being Good and Doing Good,* individually or in a group, will help save the church from the kind of moralistic teaching that is less than spiritual and inspiring. It challenges Christians to relate moral law and moral education to the gospel of Jesus Christ, the power of God.

Allan Hart Jahsmann

Chapter One
THE IMPULSE
TO TEACH MORALITY

"The good old days!" When people speak of bygone days as "good," they usually mean that olden times were simpler times. In simpler times their grandparents were able to be virtuous. Their amusements were innocent. The world was less cluttered with distractions. In a little red schoolhouse teachers used McGuffey's readers to help a new generation learn to spell and read. While doing so, these teachers and books taught the children to be moral.

Down the road from the little red schoolhouse there probably was a bigger white church with a white fence around it. The horses pulling the family buggy knew the way to the church. Inside that church, in the company of relatives and neighbors, children were taught the word of a God who was good, a God who made them good and wanted them to act properly.

The "good old days" was the world of grandparents. This world, it is supposed, was better than our own. Such a world exists in many minds, but only in minds. The history books know nothing about it. The records show that life in the past was often brutal and violent. On the frontier the saloons outnumbered the churches. Delinquent little ruffians found thousands of ways to plague teachers and parents. Armies fought each other across the boundaries of North and South with a cruelty people know only when brother fights brother.

People talk about "the good old days" of senior generations in a simple spirit of nostalgia. What they are doing is using the rust of memory, not the real steel of remembering. Surface impressions crowd out life as it really was. Nostalgic people remember the happy songs of the 1920s without recalling that they were sung in speakeasies where crime dominated. They think of the 1930s in terms of the Sunday comics their grandparents passed on to them, not in terms of the cruel Depression.

For nostalgic people the 1940s mean the Andrew Sisters and bobby sox without World War II. The 1950s mean convertibles and new homes in the suburbs, not hot arguments over Senator McCarthy or a cold war.

Just as often, the good old days come to mind when people talk about how hard it is to be moral today. Back then the school and church and home worked together to produce good values and strong virtues, people think. If only we could go back to what was good then, get rid of complex things and bad people, and know what to teach children in order to get them to act well! If the young won't act well, crime will increase, honesty will disappear, more conflict will come, and the world will hurry to hell. In short: Past generations were good and taught goodness. If only . . .

Now take another image of life in an older generation: America is great because she is good. From time to time presidents of the United States intone such a theme. They are not making it up. Alexis de Tocqueville, a French visitor to the United States in the 1830s, stated this; and history books—or more probably speech writers using books of quotations—passed it on to the presidents.

Images of goodness

What did the phrase mean, and why do leaders like to use it? Tocqueville, who found much to worry about in the

United States, also saw much to admire. He found people transplanted from Europe bringing along some of the best qualities of the old country. They took what their parents had taught them and tamed a new environment.

The immigrants also built churches and schools. The sermons, according to the French visitor, were not well designed to teach doctrine, but they certainly showed that preachers were good at passing on advice about morals. No matter what the denomination, no matter what the other reasons for its existence, no matter what its doctrines about God, the church existed in order to produce citizens who kept the laws and were industrious.

As long as America was good, it could be great. The nation had a mission in the world. Sometimes that mission meant it had to become moral. Once upon a time morality added up to a need to end human bondage, to free slaves. On another occasion the American mission to be good got it into a world war "to make the world safe for democracy." Being good contributed to greatness when America was moral enough to extend to all its citizens the civil rights granted by its constitution. When it enlarges justice and freedom and care for others, America is good. That means it is great.

Presidents use the language of greatness and goodness in order to get people in their own generation to take pride in themselves. Only then, the leaders believe, will they make sacrifices in their own time. Or they will at least vote for the candidate who creates the impression that he or she is virtuous.

Notice the tense. It does not say that America *was* good, but that America *is* good. Now. The theme has certain qualities that people can return to and trade on in order to make this a better place to be. These qualities came from the past, to be sure. Forebears lived right; heroes died for the country; great ideas and beliefs were part of the land. Now a new generation has inherited the legacy and must prepare to pass it on.

There is one more tense. "The good old days" is talk about the past. "America is good" is a reference to the present. As for the future? Sometimes people are concerned only about a future of a few hours. "Be good!" says the parent—let's picture the mother—as she leaves for an evening out. "Be good" means go to bed on time, don't cry, don't steal cookies, don't bother the baby-sitter, don't watch bad television shows—in short, do good things and avoid bad ones. Act properly.

In such a situation the mother assumes a certain quality of being in expecting the child to display certain qualities of action. Behind "Be good!" is a whole way of life. It means: "Your father and I taught you right from wrong. At church and Sunday school you have started to learn stories of how God is good, and you are expected to be good. You have plenty of examples. Now the future belongs to you, at least for a few hours. Do the right things."

To the teenagers heading off to a party, the parent who says "Be good!" is saying, "Don't have a beer; don't smoke pot; don't get into trouble." Even where the parental generation has not passed on a good example, it has done more than enough scolding on the basis of inherited ways of life.

Transmitting the good

"Be good" also are words that a class in school or college talks about when ideals and values from the ancient past, from Greek philosophers or the Bible, come to mind. These can be projected into long futures: Keep civilization going. Create good societies. Learn what to teach your children. Such references to fictional but cherished pasts, partly phony presents, and worried-about futures are just a few examples we can use to show that generations care about passing on good ways of life—or that if they don't care, they ought to care.

Some people, informed by the Bible, know how wickedness seems almost to be hereditary. The jealous God of Israel, though also a God of steadfast love and mercy, visited "the iniquity of the fathers upon the children to the third and fourth generation" of those who hated God (Exodus 20:5). But there was also mercy shown to the generations of those who loved God. Though sin was passed on from the first parents to all children of later generations, those who loved God and God's good ways of life made it possible for their offspring to live a good life and to teach their offspring in turn.

One does not need stern Bible quotations or biblical promises as reasons to think about passing on morality. In the world that scholars used to call primitive, the world of tribes, most public actions were designed to permit grandparents to transmit what they believed to be good. Their means were usually some kind of rites. Adolescents spent years being initiated into the adult ways. Not all of those ways may have looked good to observers, and few of them belong in other kinds of societies. Yet they were occasions when bearded sages and wizened old grandmothers could tell stories about their gods and heroes and thereby helped children incorporate them into their lives.

In more complex societies throughout human history people have found other ways to pass on morality. They may have paid less attention to the rites of initiation. The dances for war or peace and family living quieted. Instead, elders taught principles from Plato or Aristotle, examples from Moses and Jesus, commandments and rules from religion as well as from civil society. Parents and teachers assumed that the pages of the past carried wisdom and counsel that young ones could use to create a good world and to live a good life.

In the modern era much has happened to jar people out of primitive and historic ways. Some adults have lost the memory of the past. They have a kind of amnesia. Their parents forgot to teach them, or they forgot what was learned. Their schools were made up of so many kinds of people with so many kinds of stories that no one knew what was being cherished and what was worth passing on. The citizens neglected the churches where pulpits had offered words designed to create virtue. Silent at home, they let their Bibles gather dust, and human books of wisdom went to the school's book sale.

Meanwhile, television, which was interested mainly in the "now," took over. Being good is still the subject for Sunday school, but prosperous families leave home for the weekends, and there is no other institution helping them draw on the past.

The importance of the past

Some people think that if only we could wipe the past away and have a clean slate, a utopia would develop. In such a place everyone would come across appropriate ways for their own day. Why, they ask, should they use old examples of marriage when modern life offers people new patterns? Why teach sacrifice when laws can keep people in line? Why stay in line morally? Why not live for the moment?

But the past doesn't disappear by rejecting it. Someone has said to a new generation: "You do not know much about traditions, and yet you want to forget them, whether they be those of Greece and Rome or of Judaism and Christianity. Although you do not possess the tradition, the tradition nevertheless possesses you."

Much of human life is made up of gestures which are not completely voluntary. We use words whose meanings we do not form, words which carry the memory of past events. The terms may imprison us or fail to save us if we do not learn them in their original context or how to use them for our purposes.

Wiser people have come to know that the past is not gone. The past *is,* Nobel prize winner William Faulkner reminded his readers.

Past approaches to wisdom and goodness can be neglected and despised, even forgotten, but they cannot be erased. The past will either haunt us or help guide us.

But the past does not come protected in a package. While one generation gives space and example to another, the whole act of passing things on occurs in a time of great change.

The forces of change

Change is essential to life. It enlivens us. We grow bored on a long and rainy Sunday afternoon. People watch the news, not the "olds." Novelty can be attractive as against more of "the same old thing."

But in moral life, when new situations occur, they threaten us. When people take old wisdom for new times, everything seems untried and frightening. A great Anglican churchman, Richard Hooker, was right when he said that all change is inconveniencing—including change from worse to better.

Take a moment to examine why the older generation of parents, pastors, teachers, worriers, and hopers care at all about what change does. Criminals and "godfathers" try to keep the old Mafia ways going in times of change. Fortunately, other seniors try to keep the old but good ways going.

Think about such exemplars. We can say that our holy God has begun a good work in them. God has helped people create societies in which something of the good in the good earth gets used properly. Citizens respond by creating a society in which laws work for the good of its members. They establish churches and schools and keep homes strong.

Sources of care

Some scholars who do not believe in God or divine truth are contending that goodness comes from nonreligious sources. Evolution, they claim, has left the human race with a "selfish gene." This gene assures that the species will survive. Sometimes it acts through sexual impulses. More puzzling, it sometimes works through altruism, through sacrifice even of life itself.

How can this be? To the sociobiologists, giving one's life for others only proves that the whole human race has the selfish gene. Prairie dogs, they observe, like to romp securely in a hollow. To be secure the dogs post one of their kind on a ridge to distract predators. He makes noise, attracts the enemy, and is killed and eaten while all the others scamper away.

The selfish gene explains why firemen risk their lives to save people they do not know and why soldiers die for freedom. So goes the theory. Being good, then, belongs to drives over which the race has little control.

It is possible to go a bit further and make much of a few lines in the Bible, in the first chapter of Romans. There we learn that God has written a kind of moral law into the human heart. Evil people suppress it and rebel against it. Good ones, even before they come to faith, can act on the basis of this law by paying attention to their consciences. Philosophers, including many who believe in God, think that this moral law or natural law can be the basis of good life.

It is also possible to see that people can crave a kind of goodness in an almost artistic sense. Now and then the drunken sot looks up at people who live soberly and, through blood-clotted eyes of envy and resentment and rage, can picture how good it would be to be free of addiction. In many a story a prostitute will remember a lost world of innocence and momentarily wish it could return. Men and women who do not profess faith in God can create a kind of room in their lives for holiness, if not for the holy One.

Other sources

Concern for good on all these grounds—God's care, the gene's impulses, the love of holiness—produces some sort of conscience and care. The fact that anybody is ready to give time to books on subjects like this one, to serve as a teacher in a church school, to act the part of the parent is noteworthy. Some people wish to do the right thing. Their actions are signs not simply of selfish wallowing in the present moment but of care about the future.

Concern about passing on values, examples, and good ways indicates not only a conscience but also an awareness that a culture matters. Now and then you will hear people say that they do not care about what happens in the world around them. They want to make their money; they want to be saved; and that is that.

Yet personal existence does occur in a kind of envelope of sensations and products that we call culture. It makes a great deal of difference when and where one lives. For this reason some parents have fled the ghetto in order to create a wholesome environment for their children. Others will sometimes go to great pains to find a private school or a good public one within slums and depressed areas, knowing that there the child has a better chance.

Also in the sometimes morally more dangerous areas we call suburbs, parents know that the environment matters. In affluent communities, bored and spoiled children may despise all efforts at goodness. Parents look at their own generation and their own crowd and know that the persons their children hang out with, where they spend their leisure, how they make a living, whom they admire, what they value—all have much to do with their possibilities for goodness.

Theories of generations

A number of major thinkers—their names may not matter much, but for the record, people like José Ortega y Gasset, Julian Marias, and Karl Mannheim—have developed theories of generations. They notice that change comes to humans not just as individuals but as members of a cohort, a group. The people in the group share little with each other except common birth dates or periods of living; that is, they come of age at the same time.

Think what it means to say the "rock and roll generation," the "hippie era," "depression children," "wartime couples." People who do not like some of these movements will say that the people in such generations were "tuned in, turned on, and dropped out." They smoked dangerous substances and drank dangerous drinks. Other people learned from hard times how to value simple things, or they learned from dangerous eras how to make sacrifices.

In each generation there tend to be decisive events like a war, a plague, the election of a new style of ruler. More important than these, said Ortega, are subtle processes and changes of the mind. Real history was made less by earthquakes and wars and more by the ever-so-slight tilting of the crown of the human heart from optimism to pessimism or from despair to hope or—we might add—from cherishing moral life to despising it. Of course, it is possible to go against one's generation, and many people do. But it is also easy to take signals from one's contemporaries, whether good or bad.

Present influences

Now think for a moment of the present period. The newspapers make daily attempts to give an account of the world around us, and television reproduces and records a jumble of impressions. Historians are busy keeping the records so that in the future people will know how we lived and wanted to live. At this moment, as we think of what it is to teach morality and to promote virtue and goodness, it is only necessary to reflect on how society conceives and values the institutions which help shape goodness.

One disturbing factor has to do with how children are regarded. Family bonds are often weakened in a world of divorce, separation, and strain on the home. Even where parental love survives, not all the world loves a parent or a child. Newspapers give frequent accounts in which we can see a war against the young. America is getting older and wants its resources saved for its seniors. Many people seem not to know that a new generation has to be large enough to some day earn for the care of the old. Still, entire apartment communities try to rule out the young, to keep children out of sight and out of mind.

While some taxpayers argue about the quality of the schools, others simply want to play them down and forget them. In many communities the people whose children are grown want to use their money for something other than taxes. Having grown cynical because of many failures in education, the public habitually drags its collective feet when it comes time for bond issues or raised taxes. Teachers often are already demoralized, but their salaries usually do not rise. When they do rise, some taxpayers resent the fact.

The public has reason for some dissatisfaction. Many people are disturbed about illiteracy in an era when parents do little to encourage the turning off of television and the opening of books. The public expresses its concern by pointing to lowered SAT scores. When high school seniors take tests to show their readiness for college, they seem to be less ready than were generations before them, this despite new costly hardware for learning.

More worrisome, however, than the lapses in the SAT worlds of knowledge are failures in the moral world. The

16

statistics on juvenile crime and the reports on violence, cheating, and depravity in high schools serve as a kind of moral SAT score that leads to citizen disillusionment and rejection.

Neglect of the church

While some neglect school as a moral agency, even more people fail to use the church as a means for producing good acts by good people in a good society. Three out of five Americans remain on the church rolls, and two out of five claim to have worshiped "last weekend." But, at the same time, church school attendance has slipped. Sunday school, to take but one example, has suffered greatly in many denominations for lack of support. Even worse has been the lack of attention adult generations pay to Bible study, adult forums, and other means by which they can hear old stories and propose new ways of acting.

The British writer C. S. Lewis once said that if you like railroad trains, you cannot complain that they do not pass your breakfast window if you have moved away from the tracks or live near abandoned ones. Many people have "moved away" from church and complain about its loss of influence. They talk about the weakness of church education but do not contribute to a possible recovery of its strength. They wonder what happened to biblical morality, without noting how much they have done to help promote ignorance of the Bible.

An even deeper issue

There is no point in evading an even deeper issue. Sometimes society does put great amounts of money and energy, along with good will, into institutions that are designed to help produce good people in a better world.

And yet there is demoralizing failure. Many communities did build extravagantly and paid well for suburban schools during the baby boom years of the late 1950s. After the Russians shot the first sputnik into space and Americans decided they needed technology to catch up, citizens invested a lot of money in the college and university world. Yet the yield seemed small in moral terms. There was now more knowledge and power than before, but the public used these to acquire wealth, not to find good ways of life.

Can morality be taught?

The kind of failure just mentioned has raised a very legitimate question: Can the moral way be taught at all? Does ethical action result from learning moral principles? The humanities—subjects like philosophy, history, religion, and literature—are full of fine ideals; but are those who study them necessarily better than others? Critic George Steiner once discussed the career of one of the great people of taste in our century, the British queen's own art connoisseur, Sir Anthony Blunt. He was also, said Steiner, a rat, a thoroughly evil human being who used his intelligence in serving as a Soviet agent. The connoisseur lied, used his friends, and was demonic in his twisting of moral behavior.

Though such outcomes occur in ordinary human learning, can morals nevertheless be taught in the church? There are good reasons to keep this question alive. Someone has said, "Religion makes good people good and bad people bad." The religious, also Christian societies, have not had fewer wars than others. World War I and World War II, except for the Japanese involvement in the second, occurred largely on the soil of Christendom. Satanic forces of greed, hatred, racial pride, and cruelty erupted where Bible teaching and preaching had been common for centuries.

Church people sometimes employ God in order to grow more selfish than they would otherwise. They use Jesus to justify their acts of grabbing the world's goods and not noticing human need. They line up for worship and occupy pews, but they seem to hear little of anything that can help make them good.

How can one teach morality? By example? By announcing the gospel and then letting anything happen? If so, what about the people whose ears are touched by the sound waves of the gospel but who, having ears to hear, do not hear? Or the people who have heard but do not have hearts that care or hands that act?

Alongside the announcement of God's good ways and good news, does one teach morality by pointing to exemplary people in whom godly ways live? Sometimes the saints and heroes only defeat us. They seem to be so hard to imitate or follow. They only serve to help us measure how far we have to go, and when we fail we lose heart.

If not by example, do we teach morality by principle? The Bible seems short on principles. Physicist John Platt says that Jesus did not give us a philosophy of life. He gave us a set of active verbs: go, do, teach, heal, care, love, live. Yet Christians live not by verbs but through acts. Does morality come when good people habitually do good things toward good ends? If so, how is this goodness learned or gained?

Significant signs

Some answers to these questions will begin to appear in the pages ahead, answers with which the reader may sometimes take issue. But for the moment we only lay them on the table. To turn the corner toward the act of teaching, whatever good the teaching of morality might do, it may be well to note some other significant questions. Why, we ask, does a generation *want* to teach itself about doing good? Why does it prepare to pass on its heritage and ideals?

Among serious people of faith a first answer would be "for the love of God." Many are prompted by divine commandments. For Christians the love of Christ controls. They wish to "be perfect, as your heavenly Father is perfect" (Matthew 5:48), and even though they cannot be. God has begun a good work in their hearts, and they want to please him. God has created fear of his displeasure in their minds, and they do not want to offend him. God matters to many people.

A second answer may be "the desire to create a better culture and a good society." Not ready to yield to forces of delinquency, waste, curelty, or violence, people in each generation want to help society value people who do live for the good of others. They have learned the high cost of "white-collar crime," of seeing respectable employees cheat their employers and their government. They consider it better to grow up and live in a world where there is little crime in the streets. Someone must take responsibility for helping bring about changes. They do.

Other reasons to teach morals

Alongside love and fear of God and love of or fear for society, many people want to teach morals because they love moral teachings. It is an exciting act of the mind to debate the subject. Some people love it the way they love good music or a good game.

Furthermore, the act of teaching in itself is rewarding. Just as one can take delight in thinking about biblical goodness or human morality, so it is a thrill to see someone else, adult or child, suddenly say, "Aha!" When a student comes up to a teacher and says, "I never thought of that before," the teacher delights in seeing learning happen. If that learning promotes a way of life in which a young person stops being delinquent, the satisfaction of the teacher is great. When those who are taught learn to discipline themselves and become dedicated to good purposes, teachers have their reward.

Responsibility, just plain old responsibility to God and conscience and culture and future, also can serve as a motor for teaching morality. Adults are aware that seniors have passed on not only problems but also ways to address them. We are very rich in ideas and examples, we heirs of the saints and philosophers. It would be selfish and irresponsible not to do what needs doing in our own time. We owe our best, we say, to the future, to generations not yet born. We can be mere biological creatures without caring, but mature human beings have to see their place in the stream of history and then respond.

Love for the taught

While running through this inventory of motives for teaching goodness and good ways, we cannot overlook another motive: love for those who are to be taught. Most seniors not only envy and scold their juniors, they really also love them. As for adults teaching adults, they may do so not just because the problems are big and the subject matter is vast and deep. The people who take pains to learn, to come to a class, to risk their egos in discussion and their ignorance in the presence of others—such people prompt us to want to serve them.

The prophet Jeremiah once said to people in exile that they should seek the welfare of the city to which God had sent them. They should plant and build and give their children in marriage—all long-term activities. The motive for all this may not have seemed the highest, and it is no match for the love of Christ controlling us, but it was something. If you seek and pray for the welfare of the city, Jeremiah said, you will find your welfare in it. It is wise to care about your moral environment. Your own life will be better off if you do.

The need for teaching

Throughout this first section we have talked about amateur and professional teachers, younger and older members of learning classes, and an environment in which texts, principles, and lessons from the past serve as possible guides to doing good today. Such an assumption suggests that moral example and motivation will not just come from the world around us.

Especially teenagers, but not teenagers alone, tend to take signals not from the past and for the future but from contemporary peers and for the present. Whatever is "in" and "now" exerts great pressure on them, so great that adults, who themselves very often conform to their employers' and neighbors' expectations, forget how much peer pressure once influenced their own lives. Yet it takes heroic energy and grand insight to remind people that one cannot rely on peers for the best.

We have heard of a man arrested as a horse thief. "Do you plead innocent or guilty?" he was asked. "Innocent, of course." "Do you want to be tried by a judge or a jury of your peers?" "What are peers?" he asked. "People just like you," said the judge. His retort: "What, me be tried by a bunch of horse thieves? Never." By ourselves we easily become a culture and generation of horse thieves. We need help.

For this reason it is never possible to draw the whole idea of moral education from those who assume that we have all we need to know within us and that this natural goodness only needs to be drawn out. *Educere,* the Latin word behind educate, means "to draw forth." People may have a moral law in their hearts, a conscience to inform them, and all the rest. But the human record shows and the Bible contends that something has happened to keep us from looking merely at our peers and into our hearts for all the guidance we need to greater goodness.

We need teaching. Only in the world of fiction does Tarzan develop among the apes from low jungle life to high civilization. Even though we may be unsure of principles, half faithful, and always weak, it is still urgent to face up to the issues of morality.

Teachers will always be fallible, never able to be totally up to their task. While studies show that most moral guidance occurs when the taught find the teacher personally believable, no teacher can stand up to too much scrutiny. But even if morals cannot simply be taught, something can be done. We can create a climate in which people overcome unconcern and thoughtlessness. We can lead them to reflect about the good way and to nurture it themselves.

What can be done?

Few people today are ready to talk about moral progress, an idea which once inspired efforts in this field. (Who speaks of moral progress in the age of the world wars and the Holocaust and while crime rises and standards fall?) But if there is not progress, why bother to try to improve life?

One does not need the idea of progress in order to make moral efforts valid. Some people accept each day and its schedule as a call to be responsible. Some Christians regard their hours as a time in which they can be stewards. They see each day as a grace, an unrepeatable occasion in which God will care for them.

So, leaders of Christian discussion, teachers, or readers of books on being and doing good can accept each day and hour as God's stewards of life. But to be good reflectors on and transmitters of a moral way, they must be open to being and doing good. This may sound trite and truistic, but a posture and attitude of prayer is urgent for teachers of morality. Good teachers also are respectful of those who taught or exemplified virtue in the past. Goodness was not invented in our generation.

Learning from the past

In order to pass on something from other generations, one must know something. What did the teachers of the past have to say? And in religion it is not only *what* you know but *who* you know that matters. Alongside a discriminating mind, a brain stored with knowledge, and access to books and libraries, Christian teachers of morality must have a sense of closeness to the source of the good, to God.

So, as we face the child, the teenager, our fellow adults, we can reflect together on being good, talk about doing good, and hope that we might become good in new ways. We will have our separate stories of failure and achievement, but the past is also the place where we can get our options. At the end of the day (or a session), like the servants in a biblical parable, we may be tired and feel that we have been unprofitable servants. But we can turn over what is needed to God, who provided resources for that day. God stands by for tomorrow.

Chapter Two
WHAT GOES WRONG?

God is light, yet people love darkness. God is good, yet humans pursue evil. God is creator, yet men and women destroy. God would draw people Godward, yet they turn from the divine way and pursue their own ways.

The Bible is full of such ideas. All of them, since they are in the Bible, are true. We could also say that all of them are true, and you can find them supported by the Bible. In other words, some views of human nature are so obvious that it is easy to come to them whether one has read the Bible or not and whether one believes that God is light and good and attractive or not. The human experiences of these views are easy to check out.

The Bible and the brain or eye also tell us another side of the story. This other side does not contradict the grim themes about human folly. Instead, it stresses a vision that runs through the Scriptures and through the history of people whose minds and eyes were open.

In order to get some understanding of what goes wrong—and what needs righting through peoples' being good and doing good—let us reflect for a moment on the *alternatives* to human waywardness. Believers have called this the vision of the good; in classic writings it is the vision of God.

The human limitation

Direct vision of this good God is denied to humans. The denial is in the nature of the case. God, being God, is all-encompassing and beyond human scope. The book of Exodus loves to talk about the appearances of this *hidden* God. No one could stand the brightness of the vision; no one could see God directly and live.

Nevertheless, on the mount where God was revealed, Moses was able to hide in a rock. Then the Lord passed a hand over the cleft in the rock, and Moses glimpsed "the back parts" of God (Exodus 33:23, King James Version). Christians have made much of this concept that people of faith can at least see "the back parts of God" in nature and history.

Such a glimpse may not satisfy the yearnings of the heart to see and to know God. In *The Divine Comedy* of Dante and in the great writings of the Roman Catholic thinker Thomas Aquinas, the vision of God as a vision of "the good" was a lure. It still attracts people to faith, beauty, and goodness.

At the same time, poets and thinkers recognize that in the world we now know, no one ever possesses perfection. Somehow it is beyond history. The vision beckons, we might say, from a future that does not fully arrive for mortals. Enough of it, however, breaks into nature and events—and especially through the story of Israel and Jesus in the Bible—to beckon people to better ways in every age.

The goodness of God

God is good. God is described as just, as loving, as love. But in the moral context, the first word to note is the *goodness* of God. God is perfect, and from that perfection all else is measured. While the Bible does not use the word absolute, there is a sense in which the goodness of God comes absolutely.

It is impossible to connect the word *God* with the notion of half-seriousness. "It seemed good to the Holy Spirit and Jesus and to Me," God would say in such a view, "that things would be a little bit better if all of you tried a little bit harder. The laws of Sinai and the commands of the Sermon on the Mount are pretty good guidelines. It is hard to follow them, but you can take some little steps toward a better kind of person and life. Light a little candle and brighten the corner where you are."

Never. Jesus said, "You . . . must be perfect, as your heavenly Father is perfect" (Matthew 5:48)! And James wrote, "Whoever keeps the whole law but fails in one point has become guilty of all of it" (James 2:10). The holiness of God is, by definition and in human experience, complete, intact, uncompromising. If all this makes God seem beyond human grasp and if perfection alienates and drives us off, there is another side to the matter.

Security in God's goodness

The goodness of God is a base for human security. Humans might compromise; they have lost their innocence. They may not be able to get a quorum for a moral discussion, a majority vote on the good, or even an agreement on the rules for deciding what is good. But they are not left abandoned in a sea of relativity and relativism, where nothing is true because nothing is false, where nothing is good because nothing is bad. The absolute goodness of God has often inspired great confidence.

Sometimes God is pictured as "Being," as the whole of what is true and good. A colonial American thinker, Jonathan Edwards, spoke of a human "consent to being." That is, God who is gracious makes it possible for humans to stop resisting and stop blocking. At their best they yield and turn and "consent" to let this Great Being shine through and work through their lives. Seeing this happen is the dream of the hungry heart, a triumph in the person in whom God has begun a good work.

Why some, not all?

Another side of God haunts us, however. Since the vision of God or of goodness lies beyond history and across the gap that separates the human from the divine, the good God becomes obscured. Consequently, the person who is conscious of a holy God can think of another aspect of divine disclosure: The divine Holiness visits sins of fathers on children until the third and fourth generation. How fair is that? God seems capricious. Why do some people get glimpses of God's glory—at least views of the "back parts"—while others stumble and are lost in their search?

The deepest Christian thinkers have pondered this question: Why does God's goodness grasp some people and not others? Why do some seem to serve as transparencies, so that when others look at their lives, they see something of divine goodness in a horrible world? Why are other people opaque, blocking that view of divine good? While thinkers have posed the questions and addressed them, they have never satisfactorily answered them in their own terms. But they have found other terms, straight from the Bible, for addressing the questions.

The promises of God

Throughout the drama of human history in the Bible, God never hoarded goodness. The good ways, ways which mean care of one's neighbor and concern for justice, were not to be lost. God shared them and wanted human participation. The original divine intention was clear from the first pages of the Hebrew Scriptures. God created, looked, and saw that creation was good.

When humans turned against God's design and corrupted creation, their evil did not have the last word. God made covenants with his people, with Abraham and his descendants. In Jesus Christ God visited the human race with perfect, divine goodness embodied in a recognizable form. In raising Jesus from the dead, God helped bring about the first days and ways of a new creation. In that new creation, despite present appearances, there is the promise of a new heaven and a new earth.

Christians live by this vision. Abraham, one of the pioneers of faith in the God Yahweh, responded to God's call to seek a new life, a city of God. In the Land of Promise he only owned enough land for his wife's grave, but he lived in that land freely and for the sake of goodness because he had his eye on the heavenly city, the city whose builder and maker is God.

Without a vision the people perish. So God gave prophets who kept the vision alive. Such visions have the function of picturing something of what "the good" looks like in the midst of a world that will never let it fully appear.

A biblical picture

Consider a biblical sample of the vision. In Isaiah 11 there is a portrayal of an earth that would be fair, a society in which goodness could exist. The Christian church sees this vision related to Jesus, "a shoot from the stump of Jesse." Jesus identified himself with this text from Isaiah when he preached in the synagogue. Visionary Christian artists like Edward Hicks have often given graphic portrayal to such a vision. Its promise makes a dramatic picture:

The wolf shall dwell with the lamb,
    and the leopard shall lie down with the kid,

and the calf and the lion and fatling together,
  and a little child shall lead them.
The cow and the bear shall feed;
  their young shall lie down together;
  and the lion shall eat straw like the ox.
The sucking child shall play over the hole of the asp,
  and the weaned child shall put his hand on the adder's
    den.
They shall not hurt or destroy
  in all my holy mountain;
for the earth shall be full of the knowledge of the Lord
  as the waters cover the sea.

Isaiah 11:6–9

The continuing vision

In the eighth century before Christ, something had gone
wrong in Jerusalem. The goodness of God was not visible
in the day-to-day life of the people. The Middle East
seemed as unsettled and warring as it is today. Beyond the
strife there had to be a vision of justice and peace. God
was moral perfection. Faith called people to this God.
Messiah would come. A remnant would remain.

The images dazzle and confuse like bits of mosaic that
only have begun to come together. What good does it do
for us if the wolf and the lamb do not dwell together, if the
leopard and the kid cannot lie together in our time, if the
little child, instead of leading, is sucked up into evil and is
exploited and killed? What has become of the holy mountain? Will knowledge of the Lord spread on the earth? Has
this vision anything to do with real history?

At the very least, it has to do with the people who believe
in God and who occupy time and space in real history.
God intends the good. Always in Scripture there is the
picture of a day beyond war, even though no thoughtful
person can calculate how such a day will come.

To see how far our eyes are from God's intentions, try to picture the world without greed and without ugliness. What would it be like in personal life if one never again had to face the morning after partying has misused the body? Will a day come when we are to know no guilt? That is another kind of vision of divine intention as it comes to us in the Book of Revelation.

When newspapers, television, and contact with neighbors and one's self blur the image, the picture of what we have left and what God promises does not defeat. It inspires.

And I saw no temple in the city, for its temple is the Lord God the Almighty and the Lamb. And the city has no need of sun or moon to shine upon it, for the glory of God is its light, and its lamp is the Lamb. By its light shall the nations walk; and the kings of the earth shall bring their glory into it, and its gates shall never be shut by day—and there shall be no night there; they shall bring into it the glory and the honor of the nations. But nothing unclean shall enter it, nor any one who practices abomination or falsehood, but only those who are written in the Lamb's book of life. *Revelation 21:22–27*

The now and the then

Here is a good chance to compare the "now" and the "then." *Now* we see sacred space, but *then* all will be sacred. "For now we see in a mirror dimly [a glass, darkly—KJV], but then face to face" (1 Corinthians 13:12). This means that in Jerusalem and in our city we shall set aside a space where, in the beauty of holiness, the presence of God is celebrated. Here is a foretaste of the feast to come. In the new heaven ahead of us, where goodness returns, all is sacred, for the Lamb is present.

Now people see nature, which mediates one side of God's activity—creation. We get glimpses of God and goodness through the good fruits of the earth, good government, and the productions of human imagination, like a stained glass window through which the divinely created light finds patterns in the outlines humans cut. *Now* we need the light of sun and moon and match and lamp bulb. *Then* all will be immediate, for the good God is perfect light.

Now we see the Lord of history, who serves as a light to the nations. But where is this Lord, this Christ, in our nations today? Can the Soviet Union allow God's presence to be celebrated, Christ's ways enacted? Can the United States arrange its ways so that God's lordship is evident? Each nation, ruler, and populace seeks its own ways and in doing so denies the lordship of Christ. But in the biblical vision all nations will fear the name of the Lord, and all the rulers of the earth will see God's glory (Psalm 102:15). Don't bet on it, says the newspaper. Live by it, says the promise.

Now we see a world of saints and sinners, of goodness and goodness compromised, of sin within the saints. *Then* we shall see a world that has moved beyond uncleanness and abomination. All whose names are in the Lamb's book of life shall be there.

But is this vision designed to appeal only to the pride of the saved? Shall they take delight—as some church fathers thought they should—in a vision of a pit of hell where they can see the suffering of evil people? No. In the vision and hope of a realm in which goodness has its way, there is only the promise that the Lamb has a book and writes, and that our names are there. The Lamb now among us—in the preached and read Word, in the Lamb's Supper, in the company of the faithful—is a sign of the goodness that is to come.

So, in the midst of war a vision of shalom can guide and motivate people. This shalom, a kind of peace, is not simply the absence of war. It is a good realm in which wholeness is present.

But in the middle of our competitive world we have our separate and locked treasures. These are goods that moth and rust corrupt. Where is the vision of shared goods, of a place where God is lord of all and we are stewards?

Ugliness reigns in our world of vandalism and shoddiness. People gouge the good earth, digging mines which disembowel it, and leave the wastes where forests have been. Bad stewardship lets acid enter rain and filth fill oceans, while stream banks erode and soil loses its nutrients. Still, the vision of God speaks of new beauty and care. When the creation occured "the sons of the morning sang for joy." There shall be singing again.

But enough of this!

The realities

No one expects any of this dreaming to come into being. The utopians have always been wrong. Only fools ever thought that the earth could be fair, and people good and just. The Bible seems beside the point. The national program, our personal budgets, most citizens' priorities, the catalogs and newspapers—all of these display a very different world from the visionary scenes of goodness in Isaiah, Romans, and Revelation.

How can we bring the two worlds together? Are there only these two worlds? Does goodness belong only to the future, or is it all shelved with the Edenic past? Does it all lie beyond history? Is the dream gone? Does the Bible picture the good as unattainable? What good is such a vision? And is goodness always the product only of the "saved," the people of God?

The picture becomes even more confused when a person honestly surveys the world. While there may be some signs of goodness and justice, those that do appear can be confusing. Goodness comes from the God of creation, the lordship of Christ, the Spirit called Holy; but what sense, then, do we make of a world in which so many believers, related to God, obscure what is good, while some unbelievers or "other believers" transparently promote it?

Back in days when Christians never met non-Christians because they lived on the other side of the mountain or oceans away, it wasn't hard to portray the "heathen" as evil. When Christians interacted with and had to make sense of the *good* pagan, a crisis began. How does God work among such people? Why does God not work more clearly among those who profess the good in God's ways?

For the moment let us sustain ourselves on our journey by recalling with thanks the divine gift which lets goodness appear among people who do not know God. Equally, there is occasion for cheer in recalling the ways in which divine goodness often does break in through the lives of graced and disciplined saints. If not even glimmers showed up, the visions of goodness would defeat us.

Meanwhile, most of our impressions of human life are disconcerting. Where is the sigh of goodness, the vision of God, in a world gone wrong? The keepers of the Egyptian *Book of the Dead* balanced the souls of only thousands. The twentieth century book of the dead reckons with millions. Two million casualties resulted from one battle alone in World War I. It was a battle which advanced neither army, settled nothing, and was fought for unclear purposes in a war without moral promise.

The horrors

That whole cities of "innocents" and great artifacts of culture were destroyed in World War II is so obvious that we may think we get along best when we just don't think about any of this at all. The death of an individual, said Joseph Stalin, is a tragedy; the death of a million people is a statistic.

Holocaust: This word always comes up to remind us of the systematic and would-be total destruction of a people, the Jews. Armenians speak up and recall that they experienced genocide in Turkey. The Cambodians of our day did not even have a chance to speak up. After their disaster, few were left and these had no voice. All this is as if the wing beats of forces straight from hell hovered, flapped, and sounded above the barbed-wired earth, the trenches, and the gas chambers.

War and holocaust are realities that seem beyond our understanding. We have to deal with the lost vision of heaven close to home. The financial pages of newspapers speak of competition in which people try to "do each other in." The sports pages imply intentions of athletes to harm each other. The entertainment pages show the desire to exploit and be used. Of what use are the visions of the Books of Isaiah, Romans, and Revelation in a world where the public chooses to be deceived, where manipulation and propaganda occur with the permission of all?

Our priorities

Look at our present-day priorities. The public spends more money on cocaine than on books, magazines, and any other means for spreading visions of the good. Television commercials remind us that within the past decade drunk drivers, by their acts of self-indulgence and by not caring, have killed people equal in number to the population of Salt Lake City.

Economic predictors envision a decade ahead in which affluent people will have to exercise their imaginations to find ways to spend their surpluses. The same predictors picture growing famine around the world and show no sign that imagination will be put to work to help feed the hungry.

Crime is written into our business budgets: One growth industry deals solely with security. A growing overhead cost item is theft by employees.

If these realities are beyond our control, even though they lie in the personal zones of life, then the visions of Isaiah, Romans, and Revelation, visions which should sustain and inspire us, also defeat us by their distance from what we can be and are. Where people have some control, they do not exercise it.

A look at ourselves

It is hard to picture any group of Christians studying a book like this one without holding up a mirror to the lives of those who make up the group. But there is no need to expose confidences, to write true confessions, to blab about what should remain private. Christians, like everybody else, carry lines of care on their faces. Their lives are

textbooks on the meaning of what it is to be alone, alienated, separated.

So, it is not necessary to have each person in a group or class tell his or her story. There is some similarity in all of them. Yet marvelous exceptions occur. There are charmed lives which seem temporarily exempt from the crashes which have happened in the lives of others. God is not left completely without witness.

Overall, however, it takes no long harangues to document the denial of the vision of the good. Since that is so, we can drop this subject and trust people to examine their own hearts. We ask instead: What went wrong to produce both the remote and the close-up failures?

Explanations of what went wrong

Explanations are for sale all over our culture. For instance, Marvin Harris, an evolutionary anthropologist, believes that humans are, in a way, "nothing but" consuming biological specimens. He uses Marxist theory to explain that people will do anything merely to satisfy their need to eat. Sociobiologists attribute both the "goods" and "bads" of life to our selfish genes.

For decades the school of behaviorism in psychology has said that the good was only what humans calculated to be good. They maintain that by observing laboratory rats we learn that humans are "nothing but" beings who respond reflexively to signals. The Freudians say we are "nothing but" biological and psychological mechanisms working out the plots of our childhood sexual history.

In these few lines we cannot be fair to the systems mentioned or show much evidence of such fairness. Here we can only post billboards to remind the reader of the landscape through which we are necessarily speeding.

Scholars speak of *reductionism* when referring to the idea that humans are "nothing but" this or that. The reductionisms in the previous paragraphs can be more than matched and met by more popular explanations of what went wrong.

Some say that only a little bit went wrong. So they stitch and frame and hang samplers like this old saying: "There is so much good in the worst of us and so much bad in the best of us that it ill behooves any of us to find fault with the rest of us." Popular theology says that we are mainly good, that we have only internal mopping-up operations to deal with whenever the little bit of bad still crops up. Think positively, it tells us, and you will conquer the problems of evil.

Biblical explanations

Now let us consider biblical and theological understandings of what went wrong. In our time people have found many ways to point to these biblical views. And they recognize many reasons to do such pointing.

Some begin by shouting, "The Bible says . . ." In the Bible God speaks a word, *the* Word of truth. It makes its claims on our attention. Others have said that the Bible reveals the most realistic, profound, and lasting pictures of what went wrong. Test them in the laboratory and you will find that nowhere else is there such grimness about what humans have become or as much praise of what is in them.

On whatever grounds, the Bible does make a claim. A person can go elsewhere for explanations, and some of these will be partly true. The Bible does not claim to answer all existing questions or even to frame all the questions. But one cannot get around the subject of good and evil without letting the Bible speak.

The Bible has a central plot or theme. To introduce it, let me recall a throwaway line from novelist Saul Bellow. Back in the 1960s when every social critic who took risks came to be called a "prophet" by the media, Bellow said that being a prophet is nice work if you can get it, but sooner or later you have to talk about God.

The prophetic language of Isaiah, Romans, Revelation, and most of the rest of the Bible is very efficient. It talks about God sooner, not later. The Bible is *about* the unfolding of the character of God. In an untrustworthy world, one is called to trust the God who *is* Trust: "Though he slay me, yet will I trust him" (Job 13:15, KJV). In a world of hate and death the believer is called to trust in the character of God, which means in the God who has the character of love and life: Nothing, including death, "will be able to separate us from the love of God in Christ Jesus our Lord" (Romans 8:39).

In the context of moral discussion, it is the morally serious and hence holy and just God whose character is at stake. And always at the same time, the character of God as loving, forgiving, and enabling appears.

Talk about God does not solve everything. In gamblers' terms, it seems to raise the stakes on both sides of the discussion of evil and good. Evil is then probed to new depths, and good reaches heights of which the philosophers could only dream. But any talk about "the good" which wanders far from the disclosed character of God and the gifts that God imparts will be futile.

The origins of evil

God created. God looked. God saw that creation was good. Humans were in that creation. They were good. But almost from page one of the Bible another aspect of the story appears. People have tried to find philosophical answers to the problem of "what went wrong." They give helpful but finally insufficient explanations.

The Bible does not explain it. So the serpent was very "subtle" it says in the early chapters of Genesis. That does not tell us where evil came from. There was war in heaven, says a later book of the Bible. That does not tell where the force of evil came from that attacked forces of good in the heavenly realm. No, evil is simply presented as a force that existed beyond history and is now affecting history.

Through the centuries some people dealt with the problem of evil by suggesting that a bad God existed alongside the good God. Other ancients were dualists. They saw a good side and a bad side warring with each other in God. Some have since pointed to the way evil seems to belong to the structure of things. That, they say, is how the universe, especially the human universe, was made.

The Bible casts it all in the form of a story. The Genesis story has great power to evoke response even now. God wills perfection, yet gives freedom. Humans choose to misuse that freedom. Sin is pictured first as pride, a wanting to eat of the Tree of Knowledge, to be like God, to *be* God, to leap the gap from created to Creator. A person needs a stronger sense of divine distance and holiness than most of us can grasp in order to see why that leap was so shocking to the early tellers of the Genesis narrative.

Three accountings

Three main accountings may shed some light on the question of what went wrong. The *historical* picture is predominant in the Christian view. Something happened, something keeps on happening, to turn the human heart from that which is good. Even efforts to be good and to do good are tainted by self-centeredness.

Alongside this explanation there is the *structural* view. Without being able to explain evil, we see it as a counterpart to good—a war against God, selfishness militating against divine selflessness.

Third, the origins of evil are seen as a *mystery*. How to address its effects? That is a question that goes from the promise to Eve, through the covenant with Noah, beyond the creating of Israel, its exodus, exile, and return of its remnant, all the way to its climax in Christ.

Does Christ prove the existence of God or provide a philosophically satisfying answer to the problem of evil? No. He went to the Garden of Gethsemane. There he identified with people who are victims of injustice and neglect. "Could you not watch with me one hour?" he asked his sleepy disciples. He knew the evil of being alone. "Father, all things are possible to thee; remove this cup from me," Jesus said as he prepared to drink it (Mark 14:36). And later, "My God, my God, why hast thou forsaken me?" (15:34).

But after his experience of abandonment, Jesus is the subject of God's raising. Christ faced evil in the midst of our world, and good triumphed in his death. It would live broken but still present in all those who live by the power of the Spirit, their lives hidden with Christ in God.

No single answer, but . . .

What went wrong? There never was a single final answer, yet the act of holding up the mirror gives some clues. The holder of the mirror, perhaps especially the saint who holds it, sees an answer. The more a person grows in spiritual sensitivity, the bolder the answer comes.

Read autobiographies of saints and you are likely to hear them say: "I do not want to do good. The more I am in the front lines of the battle that I consider to be God's, the more the stakes seem to be raised against me. My temptations to pride and self-centeredness grow, especially in my spiritual life. I am tempted to make a claim on God: Look, God, I am the good one. I follow your commandments. I deserve a reward."

It is such spiritual temptations as these that the saints and Christian geniuses have taught us to diagnose. Succumbing to these has produced a doubly bad effect: They are capable of creating illusions of goodness. All this results from hypocrisy. I convince myself that I am good and holy, and then I cannot be reached. I find union with God on my terms, and then I need not notice God's different set of terms.

The mirror also reveals a second *me* or set of *me's*. In this case one does not say, "I do *not* want to do good; I will be corrupt." Instead one says, "I *want* to be good, but not yet or not completely." Saint Augustine hoped that the God who was seeking him would let himself eventually be found, but after allowing Augustine to sow his wild oats and have a good time in the world. Others, like the rich young man who came to Jesus, have wanted the treasures of money or Mammon *and* Christ. They really wanted life with Christ, they thought, but their second master dominated.

Bondage of the will

Most of us have some zone of life in which our unwillingness to part with whatever keeps us from God is still ruling. It may be *intellect*. God does not ask me to be unreasonable or ignorant or stupid. God does ask that my reason be taken captive to divine purposes and be informed by judgment and then grace.

More often it is the *claim* I make on God by my spirituality: "I need your help to be good, God, but not too much. Notice how far along I keep getting without your help." When we are honest we find that some habit, some addiction, might pull us. There is a sneaky side to even the visible saints. In the confessions they publish, they may hide their desire *not* to be holy, but in fooling others, they fool also themselves.

Also, the mirror shows that I can be moved by the good but am easily disheartened. Find anyone who has made New Year's resolutions. Were these people not defeated the first time they broke one? On my baptismal or Confirmation day, when taking marital vows, when turning a calendar or observing a birthday, when being part of a new relationship, or when starting a diet or regimen— then I will be good and do good. Soon after the resolve comes a small defeat and then a great lapse.

Some Christians have had a good word for what goes wrong. Martin Luther said I am "curved in upon myself." Whatever I start out to do, all the adventure of my resolve gets lost when insecurity comes. Then I curve in on myself. The problem is that the self by itself does not have resources that help me move out to others.

False appearances

The mirror shows self-deception. I will not be honest enough to let myself know that my self needs help. The Boy Scout awards, the gold watch for fifty years of service, the honorary degree, the good public relations, the pat on the back, the trophy, the new rank—all these serve to confuse me. Others recognize good achievement. I recognize myself.

I lack models, and the mirror shows it. Almost by definition, most of the celebrities in magazines like *People* and *Us* or people on prime-time television got there by being anything but good. They were good *at* something: dancing, singing, bouncing a ball, negotiating contracts, or whatever. Each achievement in their realm, however, may have taken them away from the source of their gifts. They always have to be better than their previous act, to be more sensational than before. Eventually they become models of what always goes wrong apart from God as source.

Help needed

What went wrong? Another answer: I had no sustaining center for fidelity. If there is to be goodness, human beings need a source and a goal, a circle where strength can grow. Where is such a center to be found? Too many people bid for my attention, so I am tempted to switch loyalties each day.

What went wrong? I have many answers. "I didn't know there was a standard. Drift occurred and the moral law became a vague notion. Compromise of conscience occurred; the Bible was blurred." Or: "I knew it but didn't like the standard. It inconvenienced me, at least for a short time. I didn't understand the standard. It went so against what I usually think that it seemed shockingly extreme."

Or: "I knew the standard, but I forgot it could be the answer. It belonged to childhood, to my innocent years under the apple tree, when the world was young. Now I am a boulevardier or a sophisticate. Other things are dearer to me. I did not completely forget the standard, but I let my feelings and self-interest get in the way. No, to tell the truth, I got tired of following what I knew was good. Things went wrong, and I got mad at God. I did not foresee the consequences of my action. Now I know them."

And I lacked the will to change. I did not know what to do in hard cases. I followed my impulses. Now and then the visions of Isaiah, Romans, and Revelation, and the imaginings of my own mind show promise of a Good that bids to be followed and that offers much. For now, though, I need help.

Chapter Three
BEING GOOD

The path away from wrong proceeds by way of being good. Getting a Christian understanding of being good is a giant step on our journey, but it will make sense only after we see some of the ways serious people speak of doing good. As one looks at these ways and their hazards, it is necessary to see the limiting and even possibly bad side effects of efforts by people merely to *do* good.

Effects of do's and don'ts

One way to begin is to look at the programs that consist chiefly of teaching do's and don'ts as standards for everything. Three things can happen to the people who hear the do's and the don'ts—assuming these come from teachers who are powerful enough or plausible enough to be seen as anything but silly. If the commands and prohibitions come from people who are not able to reward or punish others, or if they themselves in no way live up to their standards, these teachers will have no hearing. The kids will chew bubble gum and shoot paper wads. The adults will not come back at all. They are free not to.

Doing good by following the do's and avoiding the don'ts can be aimed at producing simple, mindless obedience. "Be good!" Bark the command without explanation, reason, or example, and there can be a response of obedience. The guard at a gulag camp knows this, for there "good" means giving no trouble. Chop more logs. Make the record of work done in our Siberian camp look better. If you are good on the guard's terms, you may get an extra piece of bread. Maybe, more important, you won't get beaten.

"Be good" barked by a huge parent at a little child can produce a certain kind of moral behavior. The child may go to bed on time, even on the parents' night out, for fear of being caught. The sitter may tattle, and then there may be no weekly allowance or there may be a beating. The command comes with no authority, except the power of parents who may not be doing the "being good."

Thoughtless obedience does not always result simply because the command-barker uses authority. It is possible to program human beings. Without giving them many reasons as to why they are to do something, people can be indoctrinated. Drum a teaching into a person long enough and it is possible that something will be anchored in the mind.

More likely, rehearse a practice every day and it can become habitual. "Be good," the Jewish mother is saying in effect by putting no pork on the table. The child may grow up and leave any serious faith in the God of Israel and Old Testament teachings. Years later, however, the grown child may still throw up upon being told that she has unwittingly eaten pork.

Being good in the form of following a ritual law can become a habit. Many adults carry on certain practices or avoid others because they were told that these were good or bad back in childhood. They may have changed their value systems—some of these for the better—and still find it natural to go on following traditional practices even if the original meanings are gone. Listen to the singing of the national anthem or watch the flag salute at a large athletic event and you will see plenty of evidence of programmed learning without depth of meaning.

Sometimes blind obedience is preferable to its alternatives. It is better that people stop at red lights even if they would prefer to express their own will and run through them. There are laws that exact taxes. Some of this money is used for good purposes. Though the language behind the call to pay taxes is quite different from the language of Christian stewardship Sunday and voluntary gifts for God, it is effective. And we are better off with the "habit" of paying taxes than without it, even if some people pay them simply to avoid jail.

Another effect of orders

Another effect of the barked "be good" that is unbacked by reason or example is quite different. When parents make commands that the children do not understand or when a legalistic church hands out rules that members see no sense in following, young or old come up with alternatives, improvising their way around the rules. In almost every society or closed group, people find ingenious ways to violate the spirit of laws in order to conform to the letter. This point may seem obscure, but this story may make it clear:

There were two sailors in a naval training program at a pietistic Christian college. The sailors found the campus populated by beautiful coeds, many of whom welcomed male companionship because the draft had depleted the collegiate ranks of men until the sailors came on the scene. This college, however, lived by a rule book of "be good" commands.

When the sailors invited two of the women for a Saturday night date, they asked what they might do together. They could go dancing, one sailor suggested. No, they could not. The men were informed that the rules did not permit dancing. How about playing cards? No, there was a rule against card playing. How about going to a tavern and having some drinks? Not on your life! We are women who keep the school rules, was the answer.

Well, what was there left to do? the sailors asked. Did the women have any ideas? Yes, they said. There was a hotel downtown. Why didn't the two couples check in and sleep together? The sailors were astounded and asked for an explanation. The answer: There's nothing in the rule book against that.

Just as one could fill in the name of a Bible college to make that story zing, it is possible to substitute the word *family, home,* or *church,* for *college*. Every system tries to promote patterns of conduct, some of them good, without taking time to ask what kinds of persons it is trying to produce. Sometimes the rule book of a society has to hurry past the issue for the sake of efficiency. But when we discuss what the good life and the life of the good look like, it is necessary to go deeper.

Going beyond commands

Let it also be said that just as the human heart may improvise in order to corrupt commands, it may also follow impulses to do good and go beyond the rules. There are always citizens who do not simply do the minimum. They voluntarily adjust speed when that is proper, even if there is no sign that tells them to go slow. They respect visiting hours at the hospital—even if no nurse is there to chase them away—for the good of the patient. Many people not only pay their taxes but voluntarily serve their society. They find reasons to do the meaningful and satisfying thing apart from commands.

Another kind of response

Another type of response to commands comes when the commands do not stick. Instead of improvising the responses, people simply rebel. Here a kind of touchy illustration might serve. Back in the "bad old days"—days that are certainly disappearing in the Christian world today—the families of Protestant ministers were in goldfish bowls. The congregations and the culture held the ministers' children to a higher standard of behavior than they required of anyone else's. They did the same with spouses too. The spouses could not always do much about this, but the children could.

The pastor and spouse went along with the game. They saw some good reasons for doing so. After all, those called to professional ministry knew they would be observed. And such parents may have done much that was right. They may have inculcated in their children a love of God in Christ. Yet they also had to pass on what the congregation thought were the rules for good conduct. They had to do some enforcing of rules.

In such circumstances, in that long ago era, it became almost proverbial that preachers' kids were angels *or* holy terrors, without accent in the latter case on the word "holy." Away from parental observation they compensated by raising hell, sneakily if they had to or openly in the sight of their peers if it gained them points. They either did not understand the reasons for a special code for their behavior or they simply misread what was expected of them.

Just as in the previous story one did not need the name of a college to make the principle stick, so here one does not need a particular parsonage or a certain preacher's family. Many children who were cared for by parents and a Christian congregation received the Christian faith in such a stern, demanding, unreasoned, unloving way that they felt repressed. Later they kicked over the traces.

The common problem

What these three examples of imposed moral patterns have in common is this: The patterns come as if from an outside source, not grounded in good explanation or example, not suitable for motivation. The theologian Paul Tillich took two Greek words and coined a useful term. *Heteros* is the Greek word for other, alien, outside; *nomos* means law or norm or standard. Heteronomous living simply imposes an alien standard on people, whether adults, youth, or children.

It is possible that victims of heteronomy can survive, become good citizens, children, and Christians. The world may be externally better off for their obedience. Yet we are far from seeing such people truly "being good" to back their "doing good." There are problems. The norms of parents, sheriffs, teachers, pastors, and the like are simply not good enough to help motivate a change in direction, a change of heart.

Back when fear of hell worked its effects, people followed in fear. The polls tell us that this won't work now. A bare majority of Americans today believe that there is a hell. And even among Christians who do believe in it, only one in eight sees it as being in any way a possibility for them.

When did you last hear a hell-fire-and-brimstone sermon? Even the aggressive evangelists now promise more than they threaten. They tell about the paradise of success that awaits those who are properly "born again" and who send in funds to the proper agency. Threat is saved for the people who are not in the audience: Communists, pornographers, prostitutes, and the like.

When parents come on as authority figures, like a forbidding God, they get attention. Few children want to pay the price of disobedience in permanently hurt relations. The joy of parenthood comes when the young see in their seniors an example they want to follow, a care that reaches them when they are uncared for or uncaring. The teacher or the jailer has power only if the student or the victim has no place to escape. The church is escapable. The rewards there may not be great enough. Hope of heaven? That promise can be cheapened, along with grace, or gotten at some other church or through some form of therapy.

Failure of imposed norms

The deepest problems with the heteronomous approach to life lie in the *heteros*, the alien-external-outside norm. Its faults are obvious to anyone who thinks about them and takes pains to enumerate them. For instance, the owners and keepers of the code can change their personalities. Habit leads the commanding parent to be more like a prison guard than one might wish. In any case, closeness to the code can create the illusion that they are truly keeping its letter and its spirit!

When something like this occurs, a judgmental spirit results. The "strong" keeper of the standards loses sympathy for the "weak," who live by other laws or norms. Or the "good" person becomes selective about enforcing morality. By staying out of bed and avoiding adultery, the person seems to feel free to gossip, to be a slum landlord, to withhold charity. Let a man insist that others follow the written rules and he may not see that, in the eyes of everyone who knows him, he is a skinflint and a hateful person.

There would not be many plots of novels, good or bad, were there not characters who gain reputations for being strict but who do not control their own impulses. It was cruel of W. Somerset Maugham to show the missionary Alfred Davidson growling out new rules for natives and then lusting for the prostitute Sadie Thompson. Yet that kind of deception or self-deception comes in reality as well as fiction when one is keeper of the "How to Do Good" code without knowing the source of being good.

And "Mrs. Heteros" is also very, very busy. Her list of rules grows. The campus rule book follows 29.8 with 29.9, since it must anticipate every possible violation. There are long mimeographed and computerized forms, accountability and rating sheets, laws that kill in place of Spirit, which gives life.

Both Mr. and Mrs. Heteros may really only have acquired the position of parent, keeper, or judge to give expression to securities that will cover their own insecurities. "Somewhere in the world, by God, there *will* be standards—there *have* to be standards—and I have to keep them." The sin of pride often finds its coziest abode in the hearts of those who have a program and a ladder for climbing into the good graces of God or society.

Other sources of rules

Tillich spoke about another *nomos* which he connected with *autos*, which means self or own. Autonomy did not necessarily mean being arrogantly individualistic. It could be something much higher than that. Something autonomous follows its own inner logic, its own inner rule. Thus, much of the moralists' desire to promote doing good is intended as a genuine service to humanity and it *has* produced some good. Any charting of the ways to "do good" must pay more than respect to autonomous morals. A canvass of some possibilities may serve us here:

One of the master theorists of autonomy in doing good was Sigmund Freud, the psychoanalyst who saw the logic of human behavior in terms of three functions or processes in the psyche. First he spoke of the id, "that cauldron of seething excitement" which wants to express itself. In Christian translation this would connect both to original sin and creative drive. Freud saw in it all that the child brings along as inheritance at birth, all that is instinctual.

A second aspect, according to Freud, is the superego, which takes the place of parents and teachers and puts a lid on the id, restraining and superintending the actions, expecially in early years of life. Eventually it becomes what in other vocabularies is close to being one's "conscience." Third, between id and superego, between instinct and the demands of parents and the world outside one's self, is the ego, which organizes drives and patterns of action and regulates the id.

Far from conventional religion, Freud wanted to prescribe patterns of conduct that would help one "do good." For him religion was of no service because it was a projection. (This is a subject we need not develop here.) According to Freud, not doing good would result in a messing up of one's ego and thus would contribute to a loss of a proper organization of instinct.

Space is limited; so it is not possible to visit all the variations of modern psychology. Suffice it to say that C.G. Jung, who was more friendly toward religion, spoke of "collective representations," deep mythical elements which all people seemed to have in common. When people do not properly respond to these, they need therapy.

Jung saw most problems as being somehow religious. Their solutions were related to religion. The patterns he suggested may not be acceptable to some Christians, but there are many Christians who *are* influenced by Freud and Jung and other modern therapists.

In both these views and others like them, there are biological bases for something like the biblical notion of the law written into the heart. These sources produce some sort of *nomos* or standard that demands its own responses.

But the Christian, even one who is positively influenced by such therapists as Freud and Jung, does not see in these equivalents of conscience anything as rich or full-scoped as are Christian motivations. Superego is too easily confused and blurred. Ego can leave one "curved in upon one's self."

The rule of reason

Another route to autonomy is in the use of reason. One can follow the rules of reason to do good. People have lived nobly by civic and personal ideals of virtue held without reference to God.

Martin Luther, for example, always had trouble finding ways to keep his civic hero Cicero out of heaven, even though Cicero did not know the God of the Bible. Sometimes Luther simply hoped to meet Cicero in the life to come. At other times he impishly used Cicero to say that if such a noble person was in "the other place," he certainly would be located there more comfortably that the Archbishop of Mainz. Luther may not have been "doing good" when he said this, but we mention it to make the point that human goodness can proceed from rational grounds.

One could run through a catalog of other possibilities. The golden rule shows up in most religions and thought systems. One can do good simply by assenting to the ideal of doing to others as you would have others do to you. This utilitarian ethic is better than no ethic and more useful to society than a misguided Christian fanaticism. If the greatest good is intended for the greatest number, we are at least better off than if no good is intended for any number.

Philosopher Immanuel Kant gave rational grounds for conduct by asking us to engage in acts with such seriousness and clarity of purpose that the actions could become universal standards. His attacks on the "white lie" shame Christians who find white lying an easy way out of difficult situations. There are ways to ground do's and don'ts in reason apart from God.

Of course, there are limits to reasoning. These philosophical ways do not save souls, speak to the deepest cry of the spirit, make sad hearts glad, or form profound community. Those who follow philosophically moral patterns may not be given the tools, skills, or mo-

tives to diagnose the depth of evil. But we can, nevertheless, pay respect to what good, moral reasoning achieves
even though we see its limits.

A literary basis for morality

Another source of morality is what we might call a literary
basis for being good. We can look at classic texts of
literature to learn not only about the world out of which
such texts come. We can go beyond their literary form and
stop worrying about whether the work is an ode or a
parable or an epic.

We can let a text speak to us and present a horizon we
otherwise would not have encountered. We can fuse our
horizon with that of a Shakespeare or Goethe through
imaginative and emotional acts. Along the way they may
call us to entertain ways of knowing, being, and acting that
we otherwise would not have entertained.

We can go beyond psychological, philosophical, and
literary sources and standards to see where morals come
from. For example, people conform to peers and decide
that conforming is in itself good, a playing by rules of the
game no one knew were set. "That isn't done," we say of
some customs, and then we measure "doing good" by
who does not do it or by who does what "isn't done."

It is possible to derive patterns of good from cultural
anthropology, which is sophisticated people-watching.
Each society invents its own ways, and some of these
overlap enough with ways of other societies so that we can
make more or less universal rules of conduct out of them.

There are any number of human ways to think through
and explain morality. Were it not for such systems, the
world could be a jungle. Even the Christian world might be
more of a jungle than it is were it not for the help people
get from these insights and systems. There have been
noble lives apart from faith, examples of civic virtue,

movements of sacrifice, models of human action. There is no reason to refuse their light, to dismiss them all simply as Satanic or suspect.

Of course, like all things human, these systems are tainted. They demand criticism as well as offer it. They cannot all be *all* right; they contradict each other. They deal with part of life, not the whole of life. They may have truth in them, but they cannot be Truth in the way that Jesus Christ is Way, Truth, and Life—the bearer and imparter of God's Truth—all the reality there is.

The Christian basis of morality

Christians, with no pride in achievement, no readiness to have their record of success examined and criticized, profit from various systems of thought about human goodness and moral development, and then change the question. The shift in what is looked for and offered is so sudden, so sharp, so dizzying, that we would hold our chairs as they spin had we not heard of the gospel before this. The purposes of our study are best served if at least momentarily we can try to forget that we have heard the gospel and let its claims and promises shock us.

We might cushion the shock by using a word only a theologian could love. In place of the other norm of heteronomy or the self-contained norm of autonomy, this one is *theonomy*; that is, this way points to the ways of God, to the God who was so holy that no human could look at anything but "the back parts."

This God is so full of splendor that the vision in its fullness had to be deferred. This God is so rich in shalom that Isaiah, Romans, and Revelation had to use picture language to let its wholeness and beauty motivate us.

This God, in the Christian understanding, is disclosed in the Bible. This God visited the human world in Jesus of Nazareth, the anointed one of God sent to redeem God's people and the whole world. This is a good God. Good God!

When God connects the divine way of "being good" with the divine path of "doing good," something remarkable happens. Christians, those tired old victims of rule-giving, those hangdog people who do not seem to have the strength to invent rules, *those* people "consent to being" and become transparent to the Great Being. They live lives hidden with Christ in God.

There are many ways to discuss the new Christian reality of being good. I claim no monopoly on the one I shall set forth, since from other starting points there are ways to give a parallel explanation. The tradition that inspired my particular study, however, is appealing to me because of its very radical nature. So let us trace it.

The gospel story

In this version of the gospel story, the God who intended creation to be good and then saw that it was, also saw humans spoil this creation. They "fell" and sinned; they came up short in being weighed; they made rules and took pride in these, while compromising the divine life. Even at their best they were at their worst—always grabbing, being curved in upon themselves.

Of course some people were good citizens. They lived by external or civil righteousness. They could "do good." They could not, however, "be good" in the sense that their goodness, their righteousness (to use a biblical term), did not justify them (make them "just right") before God. They could be good so far as ordering much of human life was concerned, but no matter whether or how or how long they tried, their "do good" efforts did not add up sufficiently. All came short of the glory of God.

So humans remained busy trying to prove their goodness to God. They bragged to others. They were insecure:

"Are we doing enough?" They became apathetic: "Why bother to do anything at all?" Of course, the people whose God was the Lord could turn to the law of God and could work toward being good. No, on second thought, they could not. In an insight that seems even heretical at first, people in this school of Bible reading found that the law of God was an enemy of peace with God.

Why? If the law was the law of God, how could it create problems? The answer was clear. In any human effort to find the righteousness of God and willingness to accept what God wants to give, *lex semper accusat,* the law always accuses. It always finds more wrong.

The law of God reaches into deeper motives of life and never ceases probing. It is, after all, the law of the holy God, not just a resolution of human beings assembled in a legislature or written in books. The law stabs and kills. I did not even know what it was to covet or to know that coveting was a sin, says Paul in the Bible, until the law said "Thou shalt not covet." There were more accusations where that came from, and the accused could not be the savior.

The savior came with a capital *S,* Savior. In Jesus Christ there appeared the holy God in complete fullness. He was able to live the will of God. Because he identified himself with the human race, he was also able to take the full demands of God upon himself in behalf of all other humans (theology calls this his active obedience) and then even suffer the consequences of human evil and injustice—death. But God raised him to new life and to a spiritual throne in the eternal heavens.

What does this have to do with anyone today, including us and those whom we teach? In a grand biblical picture that Paul presented and Martin Luther spent a lifetime expounding, Baptism into life with Christ became both a portrait of a new relationship with God and the means of getting it started. In Romans 6 and in Luther's explanation, the baptized person is one who is identified with

Christ. This is not a magical act. It is a relationship in which the story of Christ becomes the story of the believer, who is a participant in the action of Christ's mission and career.

Baptism in the ancient church was usually, it is assumed, by immersion, wherever a pond or a river was available. The immersing helps the meaning of Baptism to be vivid. The believer goes into and under the water and thereby identifies with Jesus Christ's "going under" through death into the grave. Left there, the person would always and only know death. But the baptized one by faith comes forth from Baptism in water to the breath of air on firm ground, from having died with Christ to having a new birth and a new life with him. You have died; that is past, said Paul. Your lives are hid with Christ in God. You were buried by faith in Baptism. Now you are raised from the dead. A "new person" has come out of all of this. Good-bye, Adam and Eve and holocaust makers and sots.

But there's more to it

Is that all there is to it? Not quite; not even by a long shot. The way Paul, in an earlier outline of these ways, told it, the Christian is, so long as life endures, both the old person in Adam and the new person in Jesus Christ. This does not result in a split personality, two sharply separate persons who do not know each other. Rather, there is a change of viewpoints.

When one lives in the old way, by sin and self, oblivious to the righteousness of God in Christ—from that aspect one is always and only other than good. The good civic achievements, the generosities, the sacrifices, the merit badges, the prayers and yearnings and resolves, though these may be good acts, none of them counts as goodness in the sight of God.

"At the same time"—expressed in the Latin word *simul,* that is, while still a sinner—the baptized person and believer in Jesus Christ is also a righteous person, a saint, by being identified with the Righteous One, Jesus Christ, and by receiving God's forgiveness, his washing away of all wrong. Whenever one lives by faith in Baptism, by the gift of God's grace and the righteousness of God in Christ—from that aspect one is always and only good. God looks at the person in baptismal robes, figuratively, and sees only the perfection that is the gift of Christ.

Summary review

In case all this came a bit too abruptly, it is useful to review the main steps to see them clearly. The "good" of both "being good" and "doing good" has been personified. Jesus is the Good One, the Righteous One of God. His way, truth, and life are the good way, truth, and life. People are saved not by psychological explanations, philosophical theories, literary disclosures, or conformity to popular culture. They are saved by the God who chose to identify with them through Jesus Christ.

This identification is not restricted to Sabbath, Sunday, temple, church, holy places, holy times. It certainly cannot be located in some never-never land halfway between heaven and earth. The first chapters of the Letter to the Hebrews are very realistic about this. The plot of the Jesus story does not go on somewhere "out there," in angelic lands. Jesus was like his brothers and sisters in every respect—though without sin.

In a letter to the Philippians Paul connected "being good" and "doing good" in a passage so compressed that most Bible scholars think he was quoting a hymn:

Have this mind among yourselves, which is yours in Christ Jesus, who, though he was in the form of God, did not count equality with God a thing to be grasped, but emptied himself, taking the form of a servant, being born in the likeness of men. And being found in human form he humbled himself and became obedient unto death, even death on a cross. Therefore God has highly exalted him and bestowed on him the name which is above every name, that at the name of Jesus every knee should bow, in heaven and on earth and under the earth, and every tongue confess that Jesus Christ is Lord, to the glory of God the Father. *Philippians 2:5-11*

There were other ways to put the gospel story, and they are just as clear and dramatic. In a second letter to the Corinthians the apostle Paul presented the good news this way:

From now on, therefore, we regard no one from a human point of view; even though we once regarded Christ from a human point of view, we regard him thus no longer. Therefore, if any one is in Christ, he is a new creation; the old has passed away, behold, the new has come. All this is from God, who through Christ reconciled us to himself and gave us the ministry of reconciliation; that is, in Christ God was reconciling the world to himself, not counting their trespasses against them, and entrusting to us the message of reconciliation . . . . For our sake he made him [Christ] to be sin who knew no sin, so that in him we might become the righteousness of God.
2 Corinthians 5:16-19,21

It is hard to resist one more quotation from a pair of chapters, Romans 5 and 6, which go to the heart of the gospel story, as does the whole Book of Romans:

Then as one man's trespass led to condemnation for all men, so one man's act of righteousness leads to acquittal and life for all men. For as by one man's disobedience many were made sinners, so by one man's obedience many will be made righteous. Law came in, to increase the trespass; but where sin increased, grace abounded all the more, so that, as sin reigned in death, grace also might reign through righteousness to eternal life through Jesus Christ our Lord. *Romans 5:18–21*

This Christ is not some nice idea to help Paul write equations. He taught goodness, and people saw him doing good. They called him good, and he reminded them to call his Father good. When Jesus said he was revealing what was "in the bosom of the Father," he gave them no secrets of magical, mysterious, heavenly realms. He pointed to himself and to the ways that made for human righteousness and righteous living. Jesus was the bearer of a word of life, a life of goodness.

No little set of excerpts from the Bible can substitute for efforts to discern its whole plot. But by focusing on a central theme we can begin to make the connections that lead us toward "doing good." God, we have learned and experienced, accepts the unacceptables. We are saved by hearing the story preached by people who have been witnesses—it happened first in them—in a community called the church. There we are asked to be part of the life of Christ in the world.

Problems come with even the slightest misreading of this rather simple-to-tell but hard-to-believe story. Since all that happens in this story is gift and grace, people receiving it must burn all other bridges and destroy all other props. If something goes wrong in their grasp of it, they have no bridge over which to scramble back to God. They cannot fall back on rules and regulations. These belonged to the old way of life and the old ways of thinking. They had and have their place in running civil society and in communicating civilized culture with people who do not participate in the way of Christ. However, as a connection with God for the sake of goodness or righteousness, the laws were buried back there under the water of Baptism, in death with Christ.

When one gets all that wrong, what happens? A modern poet, W.H. Auden, pictured King Herod as hearing that grace was now in the world in the form of a child and that it was a pure gift. Herod mused, and we can paraphrase: What will happen to standards, norms, laws, rules, and regulations? Every corner newsboy will say that he likes to commit sins and that God likes to forgive them.

When this system of grace is slack, it is really slack. People who say they are justified by faith can easily turn their community into a church called, in effect, the Justification by Faith Club. Its members believe they are justified because they were born into or chose the right club—not because of God's killing and resurrecting activity on their behalf.

The assets of the gospel way, however, are overwhelming. Christians "buy" them because they believe them to be true. They believe them to be true not by reasoning them out—Who could believe the report?—but by having known the story to be true by the power of the Holy Spirit, which touches hearts and minds and confirms the story.

The first thing one might say to the person who wants to move from being good to doing good is not "go slack," but it is something more like "relax a bit; it does not all depend on you." Picture someone who for years has planned an escape from jail. He has smuggled in saw blades and squirreled them away. He has developed muscles for sawing and has learned the patterns of the guards' rounds in order to know when to get to work and when to stop.

The prisoner intent on escaping is busy sawing, sawing, sawing. When the guards are close, he may achieve only a stroke or two a night, but when they are not, he works with a furious, sweat-producing determination. He gets calluses on his hands, ulcers in his stomach, hair that stands on the end of his spine when he fears getting caught. At other times he notices nothing and no one else. He keeps working, working, working.

The man working at freeing himself is a prisoner who does not know he has been pardoned. Not until he notices the door unlocked and believes the invitation to walk through it into freedom will he experience freedom. When he walks through the prison doors and into fresh air, he accepts the life of Christ and the righteousness of God in Christ.

The prisoner, he or she, becomes a new person with a new life. The old person is still there, but *simul* (at the same time) God looks at this person and sees not that old person but someone like Christ, a Christ, a new person who is ready to do good.

Chapter Four
DOING GOOD

A great problem faces us as we move from the concept of "being good" to "doing good." Much of the Bible deals with the law of the holy God. More precisely, many of its pages deal not with law but with laws, ritual regulations, prescriptions for the life of Israel. Orthodox Jews still use these laws for living the will of God.

It is twenty centuries too late to begin rearguing the case for observing these laws on Christian soil. A great divide occurred between most Jews and the followers of Christ in their first generation: The documents now called the New Testament are clear that Christ's fulfilling—not destroying—of the law of God changed the status of laws about such things as table washing, Sabbath days, and the observing of new moons.

Law in the New Testament

In another set of terms, the law that Christ said could be summarized in two tables or under two headings—love of God and love of neighbor—this law lives on through examples and applications of those Old Testament pages. Jesus revisited this law in the sayings of the Sermon on the Mount. There it appears in a peculiar form. He stated some of the Ten Commandments with this kind of preface: "You have heard that it was said to them of old time . . ." Then he raised the demand by adding, "but I say to

you . . ." and made the following of the Commandments harder, indeed, impossible.

In the Sermon on the Mount Jesus did not provide a guide for action or a manual for doing good in the usual sense. On the basis of the text and what we know of human nature and sin, the nation and the church would be full of amputees if the text were followed. Eyes would be torn out of sockets because Jesus said that lust was a threat. Hands would be cut off because they continue to offend people who, though justified, also remain sinners.

Still, the Ten Commandments and the Sermon on the Mount were not uttered only as amusing descriptions of the regulated life of nomadic peoples or as an impossible ideal for the disciples in Jesus' training camp.

The functions of law

So what role does the law of God play in a positive way? In respect to "being good" the answer is easy: Nothing. Zero. None at all. The law has only the indirect task of working negatively to accuse the sinner, to enlarge one's list of sins, and to make a person aware of sin. The law does not equip a person to open her or his heart, to recognize what the good news story of God in Christ is, and to help the person "decide for Jesus."

Nor do the laws of God serve people who want to know rationally how they might please God and make these people willing to do so. Such a saving conversion comes only through the gracious activity of God's Spirit—completely and totally.

Now we are on a narrow ridge, where it isn't easy to move, since the slightest misstep can lead to a fall. In the idea of "doing good", does law have any positive role? Does the law of God, the law of the holy and loving God who saves us and makes us righteous and good, have anything to offer?

To answer "yes" may pit us against some people who fear misstatements so much that they will quote only the words that say "the law always accuses." But merely because the risks are high is no reason to avoid them. If people of faith, even simple faith, are patient, they can understand the matter and live with it.

Latin expressions

Whenever our subject has become especially tense, we have been reaching for ancient language, perhaps as an excuse to italicize and to indicate its importance as well as to be precise. Previous examples were *lex semper accusat* (the law always accuses) and the notion of *simul* (at the same time).

In this chapter we come with the Latin phrase *in loco justificationis*. The first and last words translate themselves, "justification" being a code word for how we come to be good and how the righteousness of a good God in Christ becomes our own. That leaves the word *locus,* which stands behind the *loco* of this present phrase.

A *locus* is a location, a place, a position. The Latin dictionary also says that it is a topic, a subject, a matter. We might think of it as a *place* in a big book where a *topic* or *matter* comes up. This second use is figurative.

When a Christian reads a book of doctrine, *in loco justificationis* means the place where the topic or matter of justification appears, the place where the writer talks about it. In that sense we are currently *in loco justificationis* on this page, as we may not have been on many others.

We can combine the literal and the figurative uses. When the Christian is standing *in loco justificationis,* she or he is in the location, the place, the position of the condemned sinner. By the grace of God the person then also is standing where the new person in Christ emerges.

At the same time there is also an opposite expression: *extra locum justificationis.* That means, there are locations or places and situations where the topic does not come up. A football player, a cellist, or a sleeping person may be *simul*, at the same time, justified—as he or she is while snoring or playing a game or a concerto. The situation of being justified simply is not a question at that moment. The football rule book, the concerto score, or the alarm clock simply do not expound the doctrine of justification.

When law accuses

Let us now be bold and say that the law of God always and only accuses *in loco justificationis*; that is, when the situation or topic of being justified come up. *Extra locum justificationis,* however, the law can have different functions.

A Swedish bishop, Gustaf Aulén, once briefly took up this subject in "The Place of the Law in Christian Teaching," the fourth chapter of his little book *Church, Law and Society.* Aulén seems to come down on neither and yet on both sides of the efforts to keep law from being seen as part of the way by which people are saved.

Aulén shared our desire to make clear that Christianity is not a religion of law and laws. "The law was given through Moses; grace and truth came through Jesus Christ" (John 2:17). Yet the apostle Paul said that the law of God remains "holy" and John teaches "a new commandment" to love (1 John 2:7–9).

Other functions of law

In God's plan of salvation, law has been dethroned and has lost all its claims. Yet in another context it has authority. The law of God is an "enemy" for Paul and a "tyrant" for Paul's admirer, Martin Luther. Both of these men were interested in seeing that all "being good" and all "being made righteous" occur through the gospel of grace that is God's *dynamis,* God's power, for salvation.

But if law plays no part, none at all, in the matter of salvation but it also remains holy and authoritative, then what is its function among the "justified"? Why, one might ask, does Martin Luther spend so much space on the Ten Commandments in his *Large Catechism?* The Commandments are only one of the chief parts in his understanding of Christian basics. Clearly, he does not concentrate so much on laws merely to drive people to grace.

When it comes to ordering the world, depicting justice, or fighting the evil that is in the world, the law of God, which is never a *dynamis* or power for salvation, is a *dynamis* for establishing purely human fellowship and goodness. Aulén wrote: "The law is a force that contests and subdues the destructive forces in humanity and that lays the foundation necessary for maintaining human fellowship, the foundation of justice. Thus, justice is not only something relative, changing according to the changing human situations and claims. The claim of justice is superior to all human order and organizations, holy and inviolable."*

Law and order

This is a way of saying that the law of God helps order the world and constitute a good society. This was the case with Cyrus, a ruler who served God without even knowing the divine name (Isaiah 45), and with Cornelius in Acts 10. These were men who pleased God, though they were not

* Gustaf Aulén, *Church, Law and Society* (New York: Charles Scribner's Sons, 1948), 56.

living in and under the ancient covenant of God or were baptized and born anew in the new covenant. The law of God is active in the world wherever people are civilly righteous, even if they are not thus righteous "unto salvation."

The law of God has differing functions in differing places or topics. "Who shall bring any charge against God's elect? It is God who justifies; who is to condemn?" (Romans 8:33–34). The human being in Christ is liberated from the law. But the law still nonetheless has something to do with the Christian life. The Christian, completely free from legalism, living in the freedom of the Spirit, learns, for instance, from law the ways a holy God would build his concerns into the structures of his creations.

The law of God, moral law, acts as a *dynamis* or power by describing and commanding activity for the service of God and the welfare of human beings. We might even say that the law itself has been liberated to accomplish what it was intended to accomplish. It fights the evil and destructive forces in human life and works toward positive ordering and care. The church of Jesus Christ ought to be the *locus,* the locale, in which people are especially sensitive to God's demands for the care of their neighbor.

Content of God's law

When one examines the law of God in respect to "doing good," certain themes emerge and stand out. The Ten Commandments is the clearest place where this law is condensed. The Sermon on the Mount was Christ's way of passing it on to his disciples and to all of us. He showed that not mere external conformity but the heart itself is involved in the doing and keeping of the law.

We also need to remember that the Ten Commandments do not come from some alien deity who is different from the God who saves in Jesus Christ. "I am the Lord your God," the Old Testament preface to the Commandments, are words of graceful reaching out.

To get clarity as to who this God is, one must, of course, turn to the gospel. In many respects it is only the gospel that is to be called "the Word of God," since God's Word saves and makes people spiritually alive; the law never does that. However, in a world of relativism and chaos, the first word one needs to hear for the sake of ordering, constituting, and seeking the boundaries and zones in which justice and good are to occur is the law of that saving God.

The Ten Commandments gave descriptions of the good way of life to the people of Israel. The Sermon on the Mount depicts the adventure of life in the coming kingdom of God. The law of God, then, is not only a command. It has a content. It is fused with a call to responses of various sorts, for example, in worship. Isaiah 58 and numbers of other prayer reform passages in the prophets make this clear:

Is such the fast that I choose,
    a day for a man to humble himself?
Is it to bow down his head with a rush,
    and to spread sackcloth and ashes under him?
Will you call this a fast,
    and a day acceptable to the Lord?
Is not this the fast that I choose:
    to loose the bonds of wickedness,
    to undo the thongs of the yoke,
    to let the oppressed go free,
    and to break every yoke?
Is it not to share your bread with the hungry,
    and bring the homeless poor into your house;
when you see the naked, to cover him,
    and not to hide yourself from your own flesh?
Then shall your light break forth like the dawn,
    and your healing shall spring up speedily;

> your righteousness shall go before you,
>> the glory of the Lord shall be your rear guard.
> Then you shall call, and the Lord will answer;
>> you shall cry, and he will say, Here I am.
>>
>> *Isaiah 58:5–9*

Such reform of worship is not gospel, though the last verses speak words of gospel. But the passage reveals to the worshiping community something about the character of God, the creating, ordering, justice-giving, caring God, to whom the believers are supposed to be attentive, even though one need not be a believer to know and follow the instructions. They have power, indeed the power of God, but not "unto salvation."

In the realm of "doing good" the law of God also reflects a world that lies ahead. Many a commentator has said that some day when the kingdom comes, when God's will is done, then something of the caring world of the Ten Commandments, the Two Tables of the Law, or the Sermon on the Mount will have arrived. In the laws of God is a kind of model. One sees there what God expected of Israel and what Christ pictured for the disciples. Knowing that the following of all this is not saving, one nevertheless uses the laws as a pattern or guide for human living and a better world.

Law and the Christian

What has been lacking so far is anything specifically *Christian* about the move from "being good" to "doing good." A book title by George Forell serves well at this point: *Faith Active in Love.* The late Episcopal bishop James Pike, in the earliest, happier years of his career, used a phrase from the writings of the evangelist John and spoke of Christian ethics as "doing the truth." Both concepts connect the law and laws of God with gospel.

The word *gospel* keeps sneaking in as a code name for the whole story, from Old Testament and New, of what God has done and is doing to rescue people from evil. It is good news, the announcement of grace, the effecting of grace. Wherever God's saving activity is present, there the gospel is being enacted, and wherever it is offered and accepted in faith, there it is effected.

The gospel linkage

The key linkage words, as Martin Luther liked to remind his hearers, are "for you." The preached word to the congregation is the gospel spoken "for you," and Christ is present. Baptism was "for you" as a name was put on you, and you were sealed into a life with Christ by death and rising, drowning and coming to life. When the minister of God offers the bread and wine and says to take it, it is "for you," the connection is unmistakable.

The point is this: Wherever and whenever this "for you" connection is made, something is turned on and turned loose—something new and good. It must be. "So faith by itself, if it has no works, is dead" is a clear statement from a sometimes-unwelcome corner of the New Testament, the Epistle of James (2:17). Locating human works, the doing of good in the Christian way of life, was the problem. Since works play no part, no part at all, before one is made righteous or good in Christ, doing good must follow faith. Faith is active in love, and love is the activity of faith.

In an earlier chapter the author was astounded, even though he had heard it a thousand times and more, that the Christian was *simul,* at the same time, the sinner who had nothing to offer and the person who was declared good and who thus was seen by God as a Christ, a new person in Christ. Here is a second such astonishment, a second scandalous sounding thing to have to say, to *get* to say. It has to do with the Greek word *agape.*

That word *agape* stands for the spontaneous, un-called-for, unprompted, unmotivated love of God for sinners. God, being God, acted in response to the divine nature of God. God created; God did not find an attractive object. "While we were yet sinners Christ died for us" (Romans 5:8). People did not climb a ladder into God's favor or develop a program to get God's attention. God acted to create humans as objects of divine favor. God sent Jesus Christ to get *their* attention. That is the gospel story.

Moral effects of the gospel

Now for the effects of the gospel in the moral realm. That same *agape* which moved God in Christ moves Christ for us, toward us, and in us. The believers in Jesus Christ become channels of that love called *agape*. When they want to do good as Christians, they do not look for goodness within the objects of their care. If they do only that, Jesus said, they are no better than "the Gentiles," the non-Christians who also care for friends and family and those who naturally move their hearts to loving acts.

To do more than the Gentiles do, to have a righteousness which exceeds that of those whom the New Testament views negatively, a person must care for both neighbors and enemies, respect despised people, work for justice. A Christian is to do this; a Christian is *privileged* to do this.

Thus the gospel, which liberates people from preoccupation with the question "How am I doing?" in regard to the laws of God and the favor of God, is the very gospel that gives them a new power to care, to do the works of justice, and to love even the unlovable.

Sometimes the effects are seen chiefly in the Christian community. But there is a remarkable passage in Matthew 25 (verses 37–40) where Jesus tells a parable and then makes a point about where he is to be found. The people asked:

> Lord, when did we see thee hungry and feed thee, or thirsty and give thee drink? And when did we see thee a stranger and welcome thee, or naked and clothe thee? And when did we see thee sick or in prison and visit thee?

And the king, said Jesus, will answer them:

> Truly, I say to you, as you did it to one of the least of these my brethren, you did it to me.

Similarly, those who failed to see Christ in the least of his sisters and brothers failed to do good to him.

Some scholars say that Jesus was referring only to life in the budding Christian community, and others question the use of the needy neighbor as the means of either finding or worshiping God, but the principle goes beyond the boundaries of this story. Human need of any kind or in any place is what calls for justice, as in the law of God, and for care, as in the gospel.

A new commandment

In another parable there is a possibility of risk as the gospel is put to work in a new commandment Jesus prescribed. We call this the story of the Good Samaritan. The Samaritan is called good not because he saved a soul that day, passed a tract, or made the poor man who was hurt a captive victim of an evangelism effort as he was being taken to an inn. The Samaritan spontaneously and in the nature of the case did what the situation demanded. Because Jesus was the teller of the story, the event as story became gospel.

In Christ

Some pages ago a reference to 2 Corinthians 5:17 appeared in another context. There it was asserted that if any one was "in Christ," she or he was a new creation, a new creature, and, in some legitimate translations, that there is henceforth a new world. The old order of life has already gone; the new order is already here.

It is easy to overlook the little phrase "in Christ." Computers tell us that phrases like "in Christ" or "in the Lord" appear in the New Testament in more than a gross of instances. It is possible to think of these as instances in which Christ is a kind of "envelope" or as a set of situations in which believers find themselves.

The commentators say that there is no single, precise meaning to the phrase "in Christ." Why? Because it means all the circumstances in which a saving Christ is present with the believers, or wherein the believers are in the milieu of Christ's grace. And wherever they live in the grace of Christ, their faith expresses itself, becomes active, in love.

To stress the spontaneous workings of this spirit of serving love, the force behind the Christian's doing of good, it is tempting to identify it with a sudden spark that sees human need and then channels the love of Christ that "constrains" us (2 Corinthians 5:14). Yet whoever thinks more than a moment about this knows that response to fleeting instances is not the only way to show care for one's neighbor and to do good. One can extend an emotion and an act of goodness by fitting it into a more or less permanent structure.

Here is an example. It is Sunday morning. I am about to leave for church. Just before reaching for my car keys I remember my packet of church offering envelopes. It is a grey morning following an expensive evening. My thoughts are not vibrant; I have sung no hymns and have said only a short prayer upon waking. The newspaper and television so far today have brought me no images to quicken my sense of human need. No preached word has yet announced anew the love of God for all people. I am numb. I am spontaneously moved by *agape* to put in a five or ten dollar bill that does not inconvenience me or express the sacrificial delight of life in Christ. I have been spontaneous, but hardly loving.

On the other hand, I may, through exposure to the situations of need and the effects of the gospel, calculate a way to give sacrificially. I can resolve for a whole year to set aside so much each week or payday, knowing I ought not fall behind if God gives me the gifts. People can count on me; I can show love even when I am not focused on it.

The person who dives into ice water to save a child whom she does not know and who does so as a concerned human being, perhaps controlled by the love of Christ, has engaged in a sacrifice that has risked much—after the model of Christ. That act is a channeling of God's grace or Christlike love into a world of need. Yet there are days when spontaneity is not enough.

There are many people who are not momentarily screaming and drowning and getting attention in the press. They are elderly people living out their last days in segregation. Their resources have dwindled, their friends are dying off, they fear or are resigned, they can be exploited by uncaring professionals, death is their only promised visitor. I am not going to be spontaneously aware of them 365 days of the year.

But the love of God in Christ can give me eyes to see and power to sustain concern and care for such people. I can support the people who work for justice in the form of laws effecting dignified health care, and I can give love in the form of a hug, a flower, a patient conversation. To deal with human needs in a sustained way is not to be content with impersonal distance, with hiring professionals for the world of depressing sights that I cannot endure very often. It is a way of extending the impulse of love.

The calling to love

Just as one can do good through structure, so one can assure that the "being good" of the gospel comes to a "doing good" by new priorities of life and a new arrangement of the day. In many Christian traditions a key word is vocation. The impulse behind the Christian vocation is the forgiven life. Some people just drift through life. They say "another day, another dollar," "back to the salt mines; back to the treadmill." They represent, at best, a living under the law of God, or, at worst, a lawless mentality. In order for *agape* love to shape my doing good, something has to happen.

The concept of a calling or vocation once was restricted more or less to those "called" to be priests, monks, and nuns, the religious orders. Everyone else, the lay people, lived busy lives and possibly meaningful ones but were thought to be on a lower level in their status before God.

In the evangelical Reformation a new insight was promoted. God, said Luther, is served as well at the diaper pail, the stove, the desk, the plow, and the easel as he is at a prayer desk or the altar. For that shift one needed some sustaining power. The Reformers came up with the idea of vocation.

Christian vocation, the calling of every Christian to live the Christian life, the life of Christian faith, was a liberating notion for people. It helped Christians make the move from "being good" to "doing good," because the goodness had to be available every day of one's life, whether for leisure or work, not in church activity only.

To live the Christian vocation properly, a person could not be imprisoned by guilt over yesterday's failures and fallibilities. Similarly, there was no room for anxiety about tomorrow, for any worries about what might come and be left undone. Sufficient for each day was the grace God gives. Each morning one rose with the sign of the cross as a commitment to the way of the cross.

This recalling of the bond with the Christ of the cross came with an awareness of Baptism: This day, again, I, a new person, come forth, risen with Christ, a Christ, one "made good" by him to "do good" for him. In this faith, each day takes on God-given meaning and motives, thanks to the gospel of God's grace in Christ.

Doing good by imitation

Alongside structure and vocation a third factor leads to the doing of good by the power of the love of Christ. This way is by imitation, the imitation of Christ. Like so many others this way can be perverted into the idea that I can become like Christ apart from God's declaring me good, but such risky ideas must be kept alive when they represent the truth of the gospel.

Christ, the representative of God among people and the representative of people in the presence of God, lived a human life. It was easily observable in the cities of Israel at the time. This reality lives on in the biblical record and stories of that life.

Jesus' life evoked in other human beings a set of what has been called memory impressions. One theologian said that people looked at this man and said, "This is what God is like." Jesus is, in a sense, a parable of God and God's ways. At the heart of those ways is the need to turn everything topsy-turvy, to think about human life in entirely new ways. Of the early Christians it was said, "These men . . . have turned the world upside down . . . " (Acts 17:6).

Doing good in the world of the gospel requires one to think not as the world thinks. Thinking as the world thinks leads one to side with power and privilege. It calculates how to gain advantages by having others notice one's doing of good. In the economy of the gospel world, only the grain of wheat that falls into the ground and dies lives.

The last shall be first and the first shall be last. The claimer for the head table will be set near the washroom edges of the banquet hall. The huddlers in the shadows are to be moved to the main hall.

In the ways of God in the world of Jesus Christ a person receives new eyes to see how love reigns. In the kingdom of heaven the "lost coin," "lost sheep," "lost son" matter most to God. God's strength is perfected in weakness. The stone that the builder rejected became the head of the corner. The most despised of humans is the Beloved of God. The crucified one is the Son of God.

Whoever gets new ears to hear and eyes to see from the images of Christ in the gospels and from the imitation of Christ gets an entirely new view of life. Thus, Mary, the mother of Jesus, sang:

[The Lord] has shown strength with his arm,
he has scattered the proud in the imagination
    of their hearts,
he has put down the mighty from their thrones,
and exalted those of low degree;
he has filled the hungry with good things,
and the rich he has sent empty away.
He has helped his servant Israel,
in remembrance of his mercy,
as he spoke to our fathers,
to Abraham and to his posterity for ever.

Luke 1:51–55

More reasons to do good

Empowered by the love of God in Christ, the Christian has still more reasons to do good. One of these connects with the themes of creation and new creation.

A believer does not come on the scene of a world that is a finished product. Instead she or he sees a world of chaos that is always in the process of becoming order. When a person becomes a social worker and visits someone whom society has neglected or who got into a dead end, that act is an affirmation of the creating God who has permitted some disorder to endure.

A nurse may have to give endless odd hours and provide more answers than there previously were questions, but the hours and answers add up to extensions of divine creation. The composer who faces the terror of silence and brings in sound can be motivated by infatuation with the possible, which lies at the heart of biblical acts of creation.

The politician does good in spite of the fact that politics does not save souls. Politics is a crucial sphere for the orders of society established by God. It needs the motivated good works of Christians who have been called to the service of fellow human beings.

The idea of consummation, fulfillment, the end of the story, also involves love, service, help. Christians are motivated to do good by awareness of the passage of time. "We must work the works of him who sent me, while it is day; night comes, when no one can work" (John 9:4). While not all life can be lived spontaneously and with a sense of urgency, the Christian steward of time rearranges life in the light of the fact that history has an end, a fulfillment.

In some dire circumstances this sense of passing time means snatching something suddenly from the forces of evil. In other settings, time-awareness may suggest that we work gradually, planting trees and building houses while living in exile. In no case does the end time remove the believer's responsibility to do God's work in the present. To paraphrase Luther: If they told me the world was to end tomorrow, I would still plant my apple tree today.

Resources for doing good

There are resources for fitting this spontaneous and still-controlling love of God into lifelong behavior patterns. Resource number one is story, especially stories in the Bible. We are saved by story, not by principle. When a couple fall in love, the last thing they do is write down the one hundred principles by which they each live. No, they tell each other stories. Stories save. Stories reveal. Stories help them change.

He tells her that he was the subject of cruel parents, and she grows attentive. She was sexually abused as a child, so her story is equally complex. He was a hero in a story she extracted from him one night in candlelight, and that adds to her confidence in him. He was a hero in a story he volunteered, and she wonders whether he is a boaster.

When someone in the Christian community is sick, an elder, in the spirit of James' advice (James 5:14), may provide figurative oils for healing. But most of the time "doing good" does not mean bringing oils, herbs, or potions to people. It means telling or enacting a story of what God has done and is doing in love for those who need healing.

The history of the church is another resource. Christians have trouble being sustained only by abstract notions of *agape*. To say "the love of Christ controls us" can become as trite and meaningless as any too-often-repeated sentence. But in church history one meets a Saint Francis and wonders if "doing good" might mean following that saint's approach to nature and simplicity. Or there is a Martin Luther King Jr., a Dietrich Bonhoeffer, a Dorothy Day—all of them flawed people but heroes and heroines nevertheless. They provide models that give confidence that we, too, can move by the love of Christ into all kinds of situations.

Connecting thinking and doing

Theology sometimes has a bad name because often it is abstract and remote, far from the lived life of the Christian. "Thinking well" and "doing good" are not always connected, even in textbooks on ethics and morals. But if we think of theology as a way of interpreting the story and language of the community of God's people, theology has much to do with "doing good" by those who have experienced "being good."

When bad things happen people ask "Why me?" What has happened to the love of God in my life—what with my addiction, my loss of a job, my loss of a child or the trust of a spouse? Why do bad things happen to people who have been "made good"? For such questions theology interprets with a full sense of mystery. It also helps us to apply the story of God's love in Christ to human life and lives, to find more ways than before to enact the love of God.

Also prayer and meditation are important in this connecting of Christian faith and action. Some people think that "doing good" is an obsession of social activists and do-gooders, that it is a specialty of one wing of the church, an activity of some of the people some of the time. Not so in the biblical scheme of life. One moves to the world of action from the fires that touch the spirit or from the still small voice of conscience or from the recall of a word of God.

Not a few modern thinkers have urged that the real test of Christian vocation today is not in the monastery, though there, too, testing can occur. Today, as Dag Hammarskjold once said, the path to holiness is necessarily the path to action.

Some people seem to think that the activist can live off of the quantity of faith and prayer that was placed at the foot of God's throne by their ancestors. But in the past the profound doers of good among those who were declared good by God were pioneers in devotional practices. Because of the way they burned up spiritual energy, they would have starved had they not stayed close to the preached Word, the imparted presence of Christ in the Lord's Supper, and communion with God through a life of prayer.

Prayer and spiritual life are not themselves the "doing good" that some people want to make them. No, *in loco justificationis* they become futile good works. People are tempted to rely on them to make a claim on God, but once they know that their strivings and actions will not effect that claim, prayer and devotional life can become a response to the gospel, a form of making faith active in love.

Now we may even be able to make sense of the concept of "growing in grace" as an aspect of "doing good." It is not a striving for grace, but a form of response to it. The believing Christian can begin in vocation every day at the foot of the cross, before a burning bush, in a whirlwind, or in silence—there to draw spiritual strength from the God who is Love and Power.

More sources of strength

And there is more from which a Christian can draw direction and strength for doing good. The acts of doing good build relationships. The more one works for God's justice in the world, the more one sees injustices that impel a prayerful person to call upon God to rectify them. The more one is aware of the loneliness of bone-numbing isolation or the despair of life in the midst of four blank walls, the more one must draw on the friendship of God in Christ and bring it to others. The more one sees the poor going hungry, the more it is necessary to rely on the gospel overturning what is heard in Mary's song, the Magnificat.

In the faces of sages and saints one can almost see the divine life. This seeing may only be an imagining, and appearance is in no case an achievement that pleases God, but it may very well represent a gracing by God. The weathered person often combines in one face the lines of courage and kindness, risk and serenity. One sees in the posture of the huddled humble and in the erectness of those who are confident the appearances of God in the world.

Finally, there is the community of the Spirit, the circle where the Word of God is heard and the works of love are first tested, the church. This community also is a resource for the acts of "doing good."

One cynic compared a bad congregation to a department store. Figuratively all the employees enter and then lock the door. In the course of the day the lunch counter people feed the tire changers, and the tire changers buy the clothes, and so forth and so on. Instead of this, a congregation of Christians is to walk through doors and disperse for sales and service.

When the Christian community gathers, its members gain confidence by receiving nurture and direction and by giving expression to the Christian life in a circle of people they already know. The church is an intercessory community, which means that it loves its neighbors on its knees. Then the members get up and go out into the streets and into the world. The arenas for works of love are in both personal and public life. Both of these will be separately explored in the following two chapters.

Chapter Five
BEING GOOD
AND DOING GOOD
IN PERSONAL LIFE

The Bible presents the divine intention for human good-ness. The law of God pictures and prescribes the good life. The Ten Commandments or the Two Tables of the Law tell what God wills.

While it may be difficult to discern exactly what the commands of God mean in the details of life—moral decisions are rarely simple—no believer escapes the main point of divine ordering of human life. The words of the prophets and of other moral agents in the Bible give some sense of how the law of God has been applied in various times and places.

Previously we noted that the law of God, though it comes with the word of God in the gospel, does not motivate goodness among believers. In the engagement between creature and creator, the law only intensifies the sense of divine justice and human failure. It accuses, stabs, kills. The law comes as enemy and tyrant to those who would use it to please the perfect, holy One. The law does not come in through the back door as the energizing instrument that makes people good after God has made a new person out of an accused and annihilated sinner.

The story of how God effects change, killing the old person and creating the new—this story of Jesus

Christ—is the means by which newness comes to the believer. The acts of hearing and believing the story and receiving its gifts also in other forms (as in Baptism and the Lord's Supper) and then responding in prayer and praise—these are all that need be done, can be done, or ought to be done as one begins to participate in the new life in Christ.

Being good then issues in doing good. Being declared good by grace sounds like a formula. Instead, it is an activity of God, a divine gift and benefit received through faith alone. That faith becomes active in love, in a life of holiness, through the Spirit of God in Christ; and from then on it is not law but the love of Christ that controls us.

Spheres of action

But where and how do we put these follow-up forms of "doing good" into action? Essentially there are two spheres. They need separate attention, even if they are locked to each other in many ways, since they issue from the same love of Christ through the lives of his followers.

One is the public sphere, the realm where the individual is linked with fellow believers as well as with unbelievers in the whole world of human beings. The other is more intimate and more directly under the control of Christian motivation. This we can call the personal sphere, various areas of private life that admittedly also have public effects.

Christians who would be moral and would do and teach good normally find the personal and intimate sphere more to their liking. There is understandable reason for this. They have some control over their own actions, and they may have little or no influence over what happens in the world of public domain.

I may not be able to make the world temperate, but I can resist my own addiction to the bottle and to besotting chemicals and foods. As a believer I may not be able to work out effective nuclear disarmament policies, but I can do more than talk peace to my neighbor. I can *be* peaceful with him or her. In the public zone there is need to talk about the terms of justice, but in the personal orbit of life I need not only talk. I can immediately *be* considerate and just.

So it is that many Christians who have no notion as to how to apply the law of God to public affairs cherish these up-close zones of control. There one can avoid many kinds of vice and can respond with many kinds of virtue, even in a troubled and complex world. If the love of Christ cannot control my own personal spheres of life, it is likely that my engagement with a larger order of life will be nothing but hypocrisy, illusion, or mere talk.

Emphasis on private morality

Whoever reflects on religiously based morals or on doing good in the Christian sense might pause here for a moment of suspicion. Why is it that the modern world, which includes many people who would thwart the purposes of God, is so ready to say that religion belongs in private and personal life but nowhere else? Religion, Christianity, and the church, they say, should have nothing to do with public life. Let decisions about the economy, politics, international affairs, and the like remain spheres with which religion has nothing to do. The only exception granted is the notion that "saved" people are to participate in these public zones of life as private persons, individually but never corporately.

When the world urges this, many Christians go along with such division of life and labor. Faith, they say, has to do with my private relation to God. Doing good grows out of this personal relation and is restricted to my personal and individual life.

Believers who think this way often tell and teach other Christians not to meddle in public life. "Stay away; it is tainted," they warn. Then they turn around and, having asked believers to keep their distance, they criticize the world for being secular and godless. How could it be anything else if the people who are to be salt, according to Jesus, have lost their taste, if his light for the world is kept under a bushel?

One Christian scholar has said that when preachers try to keep people out of the public world and then scold that world for being godless and evil, it is like blond parents scolding their daughter for being blond. They produced her!

Having said that, it is equally important to return to the insistence that if one cannot put the empowering love of Christ to work in the personal aspects of life, all the rest is likely to be empty chatter or a phony show of goodness. One way to look at the possibilities of putting "being good" into "doing good" is to think of life around *me* in terms of some concentrics. Let's use the personal pronoun.

A first zone of action

I am and have a body. As Martin Luther taught us to say and think, the words *for you* are the most important words in the sacrament. Baptism has *your* name on the covenant of forgiveness and new life. This bread and this wine is *for you*. The preached Word is to sing into *your* heart. Christ died for you; Christ died for me. All this is not to build up our egos, but to show that the whole plan of God for the human race must begin in each individual believer.

I have heard this good news with my own ears and felt it in my own mind. I recognize that my body is the temple of the Holy Spirit. The Bible is concerned about what comes out of the body: evil thoughts, evil words, evil acts. It also extends promises of God to those who care for their bodies and for the earth from which they live. Overeating, overdrinking, being sick with work, being indolent or unmeasured in leisure—these harmful activities show a misunderstanding of God's creating and loving care. Doing good, then, means being disciplined about my own body and my own activity.

Of course, involvement with my body can, like all other preoccupations, turn into idolatry. Some people work so hard at disciplining their tongues that they turn clean speech into one more thing that is used to please God. They work so hard with diet, jogging, exercise, and obsessions with health and health foods that the body itself becomes a divine object apart from God, a replacement for God. Here, as in all other respects, doing good means seeing the body and the self as divine gifts for which I am responsible in the perspective of all that God wants of me.

A second zone of action

In the second zone are the people who are intimately related to me. Normally this means members of my family: parents, children, in-laws, spouse. When engaging in moral talk, it is important to bear in mind that one-third of adult America is single and that "family" is a somewhat distant reality for many people today. The church alienates singles and mothers who are working outside the home when it pictures the family only as father at work and mother at home mothering a couple of children. Even when family members are reachable only through phone calls and letters, they remain a part of a divine institution that is a source of good for individuals and societies.

Psychologists and sociologists have shown how important familial relations are. Some individuals spend their whole lives in working away their guilt over how they once acted toward their parents or in freeing themselves from the abuse their parents inflicted on them. Similarly, when I as a Christian have a good relation to my spouse, I show that the love of Christ works well even where it is most tested. I may be an expert on "Christianity and multinational corporations," but my Christian faith becomes more plausible if I am a Christ to my husband or see Christ in my wife and do good to her. If I create an oppressive regime under the roof of my home, I have not learned the first thing about doing good, no matter how much I might advocate divestment of investments in oppressive foreign countries.

Today the ways to do good to people close to us are changing and growing more complex. The basic Christian story has not changed, but the later chapters of the plot have more tangles. What some see as Christian principles or guides to behavior may be constant, but the problem of how to apply them changes. For example, I use my resources for the family differently in times of financial bind than in prosperous times.

Many questions about doing good are related to the sexual dimension of life. A direct address to these is not the purpose of this present study, but the subject can illustrate a point. For commercial reasons the modern world advertises with lures that blow the sexual dimension of human life way out of proportion to that which it receives in the Bible. The depictions on film or in literature are designed to distract viewers from other purposes.

How can one ward off the "lusts of the flesh" and use sexual impulses to godly, good ends? One cannot give answers simply in terms that were established in an age before television, travel, and college education became available everywhere. On the other hand, Christians cannot be content to take their signals from the world and then merely toss in the name of Jesus to legitimatize what they want to do.

A third zone of action

Beyond one's body and family is a third zone that we might call the communion of friends. Here one would think it is easy to do good. After all, we have chosen our friends and our friends have chosen us, so there ought to be a natural relationship in which the doing of good to each other can flourish.

So natural is this bond of friendship that some people have seen it as merely one more arena in which to practice selfishness. For this reason friendship does not get the good press that it might among Christians. Much of the time, acts involving friendship are short of *agape*, since such love creates its object while friendship is an object already possessed.

Agape asks me to care for my neighbor and also my enemy—even if I do not know them—with no hope of reward. Natural, friendly activity impels me to care for a companion and a likeable person, with full knowledge that I am likely to be rewarded by growth in friendship.

Genuine "doing good" to friends does not always come easily. The novelist Gore Vidal once said of himself what we can apply to ourselves, that every time a friend succeeds, he died a little. He meant that a friend's successes are threatening.

We are not measured by our enemies who are distant and with whom we have nothing in common. But when a friend has good fortune, he or she may move beyond us and out of our lives. And friends may use their successes to measure our failures.

Insofar as Vidal's note is applicable, I can turn this issue around and say that my circle of friends is indeed a place where I can begin creatively to put the "doing good" of Christian faith into effect. In Jesus Christ God befriended us. So we who bear his name are not only to see what a friend we have in Jesus but also what a Christ we are to be to the friend.

Doing good in the friendship circle is a test of sacrifice. Am I willing to visit the friend in her hour of need, to interrupt my schedule for his demands, to be able to accept gifts from both of them without feeling beholden, or to give gifts without exacting a return?

Think of friendship not as a model for how one can grow into God's favor but rather as a gift, one of those things that "shall be yours as well" after seeking and finding the kingdom and its righteousness (Matthew 6:33). When things go badly in friendship, my channeling of the love of God in Christ is tested. When things go well in friendship and I do good and am well done to, then I can see another evidence of the way God showers the gifts of his Spirit on Christians.

A fourth zone of action

This next zone of action is larger than friendship and a place in which we begin to lose intimacy but not personal involvement: the neighborhood. The tragedy of the modern city is that it destroys neighborhoods. In olden days, at least in the myths we carry in our minds, the neighborhood was made up of more or less like-minded people. They came from the same part of a different land, talked the same language, and huddled together. The neighborhood people worked together, partied together, voted together, educated their children together. Their local world, therefore, was very personal. It was another sphere where the love of Christ could be modeled and channeled through believers.

That neighborhood lives on marvelously well for many people. In some ways we all remain local-minded at the expense of a larger vision of the world. That can be bad, imprisoning, a problem for Christian imagination. But in some ways the neighborhood is also a gift of God, for it personalizes the world in which people are not bound by ties of family or friendship but by the accident of common residence. Here we interact with people who are not entirely like us.

Jesus said much about loving one's neighbor. Even in an impersonal high-rise world it is possible to take some responsibility for the person in need who is near but whom we do not know well.

Here "doing good" might mean taking a covered dish to a nearby person whose spouse is just home from the hospital, or to someone who has lost a spouse and needs signs of care. Doing good means expressing Christian love to the unlovable, the greedy, the apathetic neighbor—or being able to accept favors from such persons. It may mean caring about how the streets are lit, how the schools are run, weather order is maintained in the area or beauty and playgrounds are provided.

A fifth zone of action

One does not need to be told that every person is a part of a family, a friendship circle, and a neighborhood. But unless we take conscious inventory from time to time, it is easy to overlook these zones as places where the Christian who has been declared righteous (good) in Christ is to do good. For this reason we turn to a fifth zone.

Some sociologists have called the relationships in this fifth area "mediating structures" between the individual and the larger society. The neighborhood itself becomes one of these structures which are part of the public world. Indeed, the public world is made up of millions of such institutions and locales. At the same time, neighborhoods also break up, minimize the force of, and provide some control over the large and impersonal public domains of life.

So it is that most citizens think of these buffers of channeling structures as something they can at least partly control in personal life. Such structures include the local schools or the campus of which a person is a part as a collegian. The local church is another. In it the clearest actings-out of Christian love are both necessary and possible. Clubs, interest groups, local political agencies—anything that I can find to be responsive to my actions—these are all mediating spheres for doing good.

The Christian who does not care about what is taught and learned in the schools of his or her locale is thereby saying that he or she has little concern for the culture and life of the community and country. Yet we know that it makes a great deal of difference whether or not one is nurtured as a citizen in the cultures of Afghanistan, Albania, East Germany, a slum, or exurbia. It matters if there are high standards of stewardship in a given environment or if vandalism and crime are present. It can be a caring act when Christians help to insure that the corridors of a school are safe, that the board which directs the school district has a clear sense of purpose, that teachers are valued and that they value children.

The church zone

More urgently, if Christians do not learn to do good in their church circles, there is little possibility that moral activity will show up elsewhere in their lives. "See how they love one another," people said about the early Christians.

The church is not simply an accidental or voluntary gathering of like-minded people. It is the body of Christ, wherein people are nurtured by the Word and Spirit of God and are bound together as a family. One does not grow out of the church as one does out of kindergarten. There is no alumni association. The local church and churches, say the believers, are the places where I can do good by working in a program and measuring my response in the light of what Christ has done for me.

The New Testament expects "doing good" first of all in the household of faith. Loving actions are a test of the quality of faith in a Christian community. Believers do not lock the doors of their church and then do good only to each other, but Christians, with doors open, must do good *at least* to each other.

There are many questions related to doing good in the local church: Am I abandoning responsibility for the congregation to an overworked leadership core? Am I a member of such a cadre, but unwilling to share power by looking for new talent and leadership? Is my church program devoted only to keeping itself going, or is it an opportunity for sacrifice and service? Does the week's calendar provide indications of ways to do good? Have we programs—forums, classes, discussion groups, reading groups, retreats—for deepening the Christian faith and life? Is the worship service mainly a place where Christ's precious grace is cheaply announced? These are the kinds of questions that belong on an inventory.

One's place of employment

Another mediating structure is the place of employment, where a person lives in a vocation and finds a career. In the modern world the work place is usually made up of people of many faiths and of no faith. One cannot therefore call on a specifically Christian motivation to bind people together in the work place.

There is no sense in having the Baptist Exterminator Company unless one wants to get rid of Baptists, or the Lutheran Excavation Corporation unless one wants a hole in the ground for depositing Lutherans. The idea of a Christian Yellow Pages through which people are led to do business chiefly with their fellow "born again" Christians can be a very selfish system. It represents the world at large as being unconnected with Christians, as though all stages of manufacture can pass among Christians unstained by unbelievers.

Having said that, it is even clearer that the Christian impulse to do good is to be expressed also in the work place. So if I am employed, what approaches to morals do I use when asked to do something immoral? How far can I go in compromising? When do I blow the whistle on immoral activity? What do I do if I know executive cheating is going on?

How do I give the employer a day's work for a day's pay? Do I take advantage of breaks built into modern employment or shortchange the public I am serving? Do I hold standards received only from a compromising world? How do I find outlets for Christlike love in this zone where no one cares whether I am a Christian or not?

The Christian executive and employer also have questions to ask. Some of them are based on good policy and civil law and others are rooted in the love of Christ which animates the believer. How far does one support the system over against the person? When does the need for me to do good conflict with what the firm must do competitively and efficiently? Is it "doing good" to organize a firm that demands a profit but includes little concern for justice? Are there specifically Christian attitudes and actions in running a business?

We have left much in question form at this point, but not because we have no notion at all of how to connect the business or professional worlds with the moral life. It is simply that life is so specific and so complex that specific forms of doing good become most relevant and interesting when developed in the congregations, the classes, the living rooms, or wherever else Christians gather.

For example, a Christian in the advertising business asks: "Shall we represent a firm that, along with the good products it makes, unnecessarily pollutes an environment?" Or: "I am convinced that tobacco smoking shortens lives; that's definitely something wrong. Can my firm morally accept money to advertise and encourage people to smoke?" Again: "Is it right for me to be part of a profit-making hospital that excludes people who need care but who have never had the chance to earn the means for it?"

On the other hand: "Dare I sentimentalize health care to a point at which the hospital goes broke and ceases to exist? Then no care will go on at all."

In no time at all a Christian group can pose dozens of such moral questions and dilemmas. And only such a group can begin to find answers in the light of human reason, the laws of society, and the Word of God.

The ministry of the laity

What is interesting about such questions is the fact that they belong largely to the ministry of the laity. Sometimes Christians are tempted to measure that ministry by the number of nights a week the church lights are on for churchly activity. If one had a cosmic eye and a computer, however, it would be possible to see that much "doing good" happens where Christians are not clumped together and when they get no credit for being Christians in action.

Christians gather together to get their signals straight. They huddle to hear faith stories and build morale, to praise God and get motivated, to experience the love of God given and spoken as they hear the words "for you." But then they disperse from the sanctuary. The documents of the Second Vatican Council remind us that only the laity can go to most of the places to which the church needs to go. Even statistically that point is true, since laity outnumber clergy several hundred to one.

Professional ministers are to devote themselves mainly to sustained study and the preaching and teaching of the Word of God. Such persons are to exemplify "doing good" despite their fallibility, but they are chiefly the player-coaches. They are to enable the saints of God to be Christian citizens in the human arena.

The common need

How does the interaction between the lay people of God and the teacher proceed, and how does it promote "doing good"? Everything begins with a story. The Christian community—we cannot say it often enough—is not based on common moral principles. George Bernard Shaw once said that it would be as surprising to find the word "morality" in the Bible as it would be to find the word "bicycle." The Bible is a book about being good in the light of God's gracious activity; it is not concerned about the appearance of doing good. The story works its own effect: I hear "about" Jesus, but what I hear is not a lecture; it is an offering of the gifts of God and a call that makes possible my response.

The story offers many benefits for that way of life in which one is to do good. It gives perspective, because it throws human life up against the standards of the divine. With God as both the measure and the giver, human failures to do good need never lead to despair. On the other hand, human achievements in doing good dare never lead to pride.

The Christian story does not provide a special set of moral guidelines. Justice is justice, peace is peace, food is food, and God lets rain fall on the unjust as well as the just. At the same time, the Christian story gives a special meaning to human activity, a special motive for doing good. It is a story of resurrection and new life, and Christians receive staying power from this.

Christians are to keep on doing good in the world, even when their causes seem to be losing or when they are losing. They are not to depend for morale on being successful or even on making progress. They see that in the midst of an absurd and evil world, Jesus Christ is the first fruit and mark of a new creation. They, therefore, continue God's work through faith in Jesus.

The saving story

The gospel story is important precisely because it is *not* natural; it does not begin within us as we are by nature. If it were natural, then the cross of Jesus Christ would be unnecessary. If humans could come into the presence of God, the holy One, by their own good acts, then the suffering and death of Jesus Christ would be a pointless cruelty. But the cross was and is part of the story. Otherwise it could work no good effects.

Humans cannot sit down at word processors and idly press keys or assemble sentences and call it the Word of God. The Word of God is a mysterious but saving story about a people at the east end of the Mediterranean, about a rabbi who lived among them, about a community of believers that grew, against all reason and odds, on the soil of his rising from death to a new, immortal life.

The telling of that story has an interesting effect on the community of those who would do good: It builds their sense of worth. True Christian literature urges God's people to see themselves in perspective. Human beings cannot face the brightness of the holy One and live. They cannot parade their holy acts and think that these measure up to what God asks. At the same time, however, Christian faith asks people to do good as Christs to their neighbors. They are, each of them, not to see themselves only "in Adam," as old selfish persons. *Simul* (at the same time) they are to see themselves "in Christ," where God has begun a new work in them.

Today many peddlers of human philosophies concentrate on self-esteem. People, they say, are to look inside themselves, to see their potential, and to develop outlooks which help them say "I count," "I matter," "I am somebody." Such world views and techniques do not always have to be at war with God's purposes for us. They will be at war only if we think that through them we have a claim on God.

The Christian sees that the object of esteem is outside the human self, in Jesus Christ, who is loved by God, the holy One. Through Baptism the believer is implanted "in Christ," where God's own esteem is handed over as a gift. There everything is to be seen in a new light. Some psychologists say that people who possess no self-worth are as dangerous as those who have too much of it. Christ-based self-worth is of an entirely different sort.

Some observers think that Christians do not do good because they are so busy making a claim on God by showing that they are humble, worthless beings. "Look at me, God; I am better than any one else at hating myself." That's a way of saying, "I am so selfish and worthless that God must be impressed by my despising myself."

Thinking of one's self as a worm (in the language of Psalm 22) because one's righteousness is not good enough to please God can be transposed psychologically into a sense of "worminess" that can ruin human relations. Who wants to be loved by a worm, unless it be another worm? People want to be loved by a warm, happy human being, someone whose love endows the beloved with a feeling of worth.

Life built on Christ

On the basis of the gospel story, the Christian begins to develop a way of life that sustains "doing good" despite all the lapses that demand forgiveness. One way to do this is through gaining a Christlike character.

Ever since Aristotle was introduced to the Christian world, this Greek philosopher has been put to work to help people see how Christian ways of "doing good" live on. Aristotle thought that the good person habitually did good things toward good ends until such doing became a part of the person's character. One could expect goodness from the good, according to Aristotle.

The Christian view of human nature is more realistic. Habit can fail. In a crisis, people can forget good habits. The evil that remains in one's history and is embodied in a war with evil can win out in a crisis. In other words, saints fall and heroes are weak.

Having said that, however, it is also possible to admire the ways in which Christlike character does get to be formed in people on whom we count. They grow stronger from their victories, even if the forces of God then make bigger game out of them and attack them harder. Parents are not wasting time in developing their own good character. They and teachers of children are putting time to good use when they try to model and inculcate good habits.

This view does not settle everything. But it does mean that one need not call an ecumenical council to make every moral decision in respect to human activities or priorities. Rather, one can draw on the character that is maturing into the ways of Christ.

In private life as elsewhere the Christian is perfectly free to relate the Christian story and Christian motivation to human systems of doing good. Thomas Jefferson has much to say to the Christian who is in pursuit of equality and justice, even though Jefferson stood far from Jesus Christ as the basis for "doing good." John Stuart Mill does not lead the Christian astray when he asks for the greatest good for the greatest number.

After the story is learned and character has been nurtured, the Christian does not come to the point of saying, "Now I have reached the realm where I do only good." Rather, growth in grace, works of love, and freedom to do good improve the eye by which believers examine themselves and can see human need beyond themselves.

Grace and peace

At the end of a day, Christians of good character, having seen the way God's law depicts justice and care and the way Christ's love motivates responses, know more about the gap between God and humans than ever before. Especially then comes a turning and returning to the throne of grace as they turn the unfinished, flawed day over to God, who uses it as the raw materials of another day.

When the new day comes, the Christian does not rise and enter the world with answers to all of its problems. The Christian makes or looks on the sign of the cross as the signal of the baptized and forgiven life and comes forth refreshed as a new person. That person walks in the midst of the world, reflecting Jesus who did the same.

Chapter Six
BEING GOOD
AND DOING GOOD
IN PUBLIC LIFE

Most Christians can see how to relate Christian faith to doing good in their personal lives. The believer thinks: I have some control of the virtues and vices of my own bodily existence and can let the love of Christ inform and direct my private life. I can cope with my family, choose my friends, serve my neighborhood, and make an impact on my work place. I can also take a responsible part in my congregation's life and can learn growth in grace there.

Mention public life and the Christian often grows confused about how to relate the Christian faith and the doing of good to it. On one level the difficulty may not be great, since *public* can simply mean the theatre in which the believer works out personal faith and life. Thus we speak of Jesus' "public ministry." He did not do his works of love only in synagogues or in his Temple visits. Jesus ministered to others in the forum, the council, the marketplace, in boats, and while walking furrows. He was being and doing good in public.

Public, however, usually has an additional and more jarring meaning. Here things grow more complex. By most definitions *public* involves the stranger and the strange group. The Christian church by definition and by nature is made up of those who are responsive to the gospel of Jesus Christ and are called by his name. The public is made up of Christians, Jews, agnostics, Buddhists, Platonists, the ignorant, the uncaring, the ethical, the sacrificial, those who have clear philosophies, and those who have none.

The public may be friendly to the Christian faith and to Christians and the Christian church. After all, through the centuries Christians have helped produce the institutions and thought-world of the public, and thus they get some return back by way of favor. But in the modern world, as in the Greco-Roman world of Christian origins, the civil state and the public order are not constituted only by people living in Christ.

That fact changes things so far as "doing good" is concerned. Christian motives may remain the same: One does good out of a heart that is made good by Christ's acts and gifts. But choices, actions, and ways of following up on both—all these grow more difficult the more "public" the public is. We must face this problem frankly, especially since much of public life is considered to be an order of God. The church has trouble working out the Christlike way of doing good in that order.

Separation of church and state

The polls show that most Americans cherish the separation of church and state. They do not want the civil realm to intrude on the church, as it does in all totalitarian societies. Citizens do not want some churches to be established or to have privileges at the expense of others. Most

thoughtful Christians do not want to dominate public life at the expense of those who are not Christian.

Thomas Jefferson once wrote that whether a neighbor believes in twenty gods, one god, or no gods, he can be a full citizen so long as he does not rob me, break my leg, or live lawlessly. The United States Constitution assures that our society does not legally and officially "tilt" toward religion or a particular religion. That principle determines the rules of the game. To tamper with it might mean tearing up a cherished fabric of our American way of life.

So, "Don't meddle in public life," most Americans tell their church leaders. They have seen religion too often misused to inspire holy wars. They have seen unrepresentative bureaus and boards speak for believers in the political realm. They have resented street demonstrations by religious agitators for policies with which they do not agree. They have seen risks even in publicly suppporting policies with which they agree. They fear that these will alienate from Christ the people who disagree with the Christians who demonstrate.

Having said all that, however, Christian people at the same time give evidence of seeing that the public and political orders *are* scenes of moral activity. They pass laws to effect good ways of life. They prosecute and imprison officials who are found "not doing good." They know that through political life one can work against the purposes of God.

More people are killed through public policies that have gone wrong than by private vices. Citizens can act selfishly or ignorantly and be aggressors in war. They can fail to work for order and permit criminality. They can fail to supervise nursing homes and can thereby contribute to the indignity and death of aged people.

Bad public policies can help produce bad people when these give license to cheating or encouragement to the works of injustice. It is immoral and not Christlike to close one's eyes to injustices in public life, to put religious faith in a safe little compartment, or to ignore human need. Somehow Christians must make connections between personal faith and public life.

The public order

The first step to be taken in making connections between belief and action is to see what the political order is. As careful political scientists point out, politics is a very limited order. It represents a modest but crucial science that the Christian sees as being "under God" and the lordship of Jesus Christ. Politics may reflect both the Ten Commandments and the best of human reason, but politics does not reach the deepest needs of the human heart. It does not satisfy the search for God or give life to the experience of Christ. Politics does not save souls or make sad hearts glad.

Politics is the name we give to a concern for the human *polis*, the Greek word for city, for public affairs united in civil order. It lives off disagreement, argument, and attempts by groups to assert power. At its best, it helps reduce the violence that seems to be history's dirty and open secret. In place of violence it invents rules whereby people seek to persuade each other.

Politically, people elect representatives and vote on policies. From this restrained way of dealing with conflicting interests, there is always a goal of compromise, in which some measure of justice is done, some measure of self-interest is satisfied, and some good can come, even if not all parties can have their way.

In these terms the Christian sees the political arena to be a fruitful place for faithful stewardship and service. The stakes there are high and the temptations are great. The illusions of power grow with the political power one gains. The nations of the world and the rulers take counsel, says

Psalm 2, and then they turn prideful and forgetful of God. But "he who sits in the heavens laughs" and shall hold the politically proud "in derision."

The power of politics

The power of politics can lead to idolatry. One can turn the political society into nothing but a political society and look to it for all entitlements and solutions. This makes politics into one more idol. Such a result is even worse than not granting the political order the status that the Bible grants it, that of an instrument of God for good (Romans 13:4).

Once one limits the scope of politics, it is possible to be free to do Christian actions alongside the non-Christians in political life. A Christian is free to "do good" out of the heart that has been declared righteous and has become good. This does not mean that pure and perfect actions are possible. Politics in particular often reveals the taint of human self-interest. But in its sphere many people rise above self-interest for the good of the commonwealth. Good things have come through political action.

The problem in political action

The problem for the church is that political action is common, united action. Most good policies and candidates attract non-Christians as well as Christians, and the church itself is not a gathering of politically like-minded people. In other words, Christian faith unites Republicans and Democrats, the Left and the Right, Conservatives and Liberals, the apathetic and the pathetic; all are united by their need for God's love and their joy in Christ's gifts.

There is special power when Christians *can* get together to effect change over against injustice. But there is great risk. Some people may be estranged from the church and the love of God if they disagree, as they legitimately may and must, over a political action of a particular Christian group. Politically active Christians often identify their own finite positions with the knowledge of an infinitely wise God.

Christians may think they can pass by the problem by never taking a stand, but that approach doesn't work either. Many Christians in Germany in the 1930s said that they were private believers, not public or political persons, and that they simply would take no stand for or against Nazism, Hitler, or the extermination of the Jews. Hitler knew then that he could count on the silent. Not to take a stand is to take a stand.

Some consensus, but . . .

In retrospect, most Christians will say that the support of the ending of human slavery was a long overdue, biblically founded political act. It is not hard to see why Christian consciences later could be rallied to assure basic civil rights to those who were offered rights by the United States Constitution and were denied them by unjust practices and local laws. These were easy cases, even if they looked hard in their time.

But most political issues do not appear in such easy "good" and "bad" terms. Very often much can be said on several sides of an issue by Christians who cannot claim complete knowledge of a sure application of the will of God.

Unclear issues

Here is an illustration. The biblical command to feed the world stirs in the Christian a response to share bread with the hungry. The question is how? Simply to give, ship, and send food to a nation in hardship is not always the best solution. Christians want to do good, and yet they may help breed corruption among leaders of the receiving nations. Furthermore, helping the poor may breed dependency.

So the Christian politically decides that a better policy is to send agronomists, volunteers, and teachers to bring tools and fertilizers and better farming methods to people in need. Thereupon the people can develop their own economy and grow independent.

The experts say that not to use certain chemicals and pesticides will mean the spreading of hunger. But other experts have found that some of these pesticides cause cancer. There seem to be no good alternatives in this situation. Do we do nothing, therefore, or hold a debating council; or must we move in support of one policy or the other?

It is possible to make a list of such ambiguous issues in just as crucial a matter as national defense. One can be a simple pacifist out of love for Christ, but ordinarily most Christians see the possibility of some legitimate sort of defense. They also quickly learn that in our mad modern world, defense can breed its own spirits and ethos. Preparedness and weaponry become our idols.

How much money shall a country invest in weaponry? How much shall we let the martial spirit of our country take over our hearts? How Christian is it to see our own nation in perfect terms and another nation in demonic terms? How helpful? How much energy can we rightly put into conciliatory activity at the risk of being naive? At what point does disarmament activity make our country vulnerable? Is the Christian to say nothing and let Mars and Chaos have their own ways unchallenged?

As in the case of business ethics in the previous chapter, so here, too, we are interested only in posing how questions may come up. This is not a book on pesticides or nuclear weapons. This is a book to help us think about ways to pass along concepts of "doing good" in the circle of those who are "being good." So here we are envisioning some ways to channel Christian impulses in the political and public realms.

A basic guideline

One safe guideline is to say that the church dare never be less concrete than the Bible and not so concrete as to say "Support this candidate" or "Put all your energies into this policy."

The Bible is nothing but concrete. Read the prophets. They do not speak about principles of justice, but about evil kings by name. The Bible uses words like *widow* and *orphan* and *landlord*. On the other hand, when the Christian church is too sure that it can take these concrete directions and channel all of the members of a Christian community into support of one solution to an issue, it soon may draw its life from the political order, not from the Word of God. It makes absolutes out of the partial and the relative. That turns policies into idols.

Doing good through political action

Having urged passion for the concrete and caution about over-precision in the politically concrete, it is necessary to move into seeing how public and political action fit into the Christian scheme of doing good. Often Christians who do not connect the two abandon the public realm to Satan.

Only church matters fuse the two spheres for such Christians. They sometimes want to pass laws that will make the state give privilege to religion, their own religion. They want theirs to be an officially "Christian America," something it never was legally from the time the ink on the Constitution first dried.

If it is not a Christian state, then is not the public order simply secular and worldly? It is certainly secular, for it belongs to this *saeculum* (this age) and will disappear. It is worldly, for one can belong to it as a child of the world, and it can function under the leadership of worldly people. But the state is never *simply* secular and worldly, for this age is still something that unfolds under the creative and governing power of God. And though the demonic may be present in it, this world is also God's world, living under his divine lordship.

Another way of thinking

Clearly some other way of hearing the Word of God must be at work in the Christian believers' circle that is Christ's church, and in the citizens' circle that is the civil realm, the state and its government. The gospel of Jesus Christ is not at home in the state, for it is the saving word that kills and then gives life through faith in Jesus Christ. The state may welcome it or, without welcoming it, may benefit from Christian participation in the state.

However, the state cannot use the mercy of God in Christ, his forgiving love, as the key to its rule. The state is to be concerned with the justice of God and the pursuit of human welfare either as Christians see it or as the constitutions of free societies which include Christians see it. In the political and public realm one can do good with or without Christian faith.

The Bible makes room for leadership by nonbelievers and for civil alliance and actions of Christians with non-Christians. God still orders the world and has a word which helps to constitute and govern and regulate it. And Christians can and do participate in the realm where all that occurs.

It may also be that Christian awareness of a need to do good in the public and political order will be less needed in the future than in the past and present. At the time of his prime, Martin Luther King Jr. was not only interested in changing laws but in changing hearts, so there would be understanding and support for better laws. Out of all this could grow a world in which divine caring would be more visible, even if not everyone in our society recognized justice and good government as divine gifts.

Therefore, Christians may not do all that needs to be done—or will not do it best—by having ecumenical organizations, denominations, or local jurisdictions pass resolutions that indicate the will of majorities. When church groups do these actions, they must make clear that often these resolutions speak *to* the church and not *for* the church. There needs to be a display of the process by which these documents get produced. Often they have increased power when they come from movements within the church, from caucuses which do not pretend to speak for everyone but which alert consciences and organize forces that help effect a political change.

Some more questions

Here anyone who waits to pounce can pounce with a question. What if half a congregation or a denomination urges, for example, the divesting of funds in firms that do business with South Africa because the South Africans promote injustice through cruel apartheid practices? People are killed through such demeaning and violent policies of segregation. At the same time, another half of the congregation or denomination may advocate the retaining of investments in such firms. They hear that to divest would be to plunge South Africa into chaos and bloody revolution. Why doesn't everyone shut up and go on putting flowers on the altar, singing the hymns, and caring for the sick and poor close to home? someone may ask.

Why, indeed? For one thing, Christians believe that in the course of study and counsel they can grow in understanding of a human problem, social as well as personal. They can gain information, hear the testimony of specialists, and perhaps come toward intelligent decisions. Furthermore, both or all "sides" know that as Christians they cannot escape the need to care. But this does not mean that every Christian and every Christian congregation can gain expertise and have moral energy for everything that is in the morning paper. Yet they have to begin somewhere.

If both or all sides care, they may very well not agree on how that care will come about. Not always do separate policies contradict each other. Where they do not, people benefit both ways.

Here's a sample situation: One part of a congregation says that we must care for the aged by visiting the nursing homes, being Christlike friends to the aged, learning from them, and helping them care for others. Another group says that we must care by going to the state capitol to work for laws that promote standards of nursing home supervision, because people are neglected, demeaned, or killed by the lack of supervision or by corrupt supervision in such homes. The two groups may not agree on the church's role, but both sides are learning to subject their position to the teachings of Christ. And if each accepts the challenge of the new information and motivation, the aged poor will benefit from both courses of action.

A mechanism for doing good

This is a good place to describe a typical congregational mechanism for effecting an approach to doing good in the political order. The first step is to take up concrete biblical-type cases in the fellowship of Christians. That often is not done, either because of apathy or more often because of fear that it will be too decisive. Conflict is not seen as potentially creative; so controversial topics are not brought up, and Christians become more removed than before from the arena where good can be effected. If a congregation decides to change, to set up the means to take up public issues, certain ground rules need to be followed.

Ground rules for advocacy

At the top is the decision not to let the fellowship in Christ be broken, no matter what emotional subject is brought to a discussion. People of the world, with or without a Christian mixture, keep legislative bodies going because they have rules of the game, even when they disagree violently. Christians ought to be able to do as well as secular minded people.

Second, provide forums in which persons with differing views can speak their disagreements in each other's hearing. Some church people leave a meeting and gather for coffee later: "Boy, here's what I wanted to say to that sexist" or "Here's what I was really thinking!" Too much of that goes on outside the circles where it would do the most good. The church of the reconciled ought to be able to provide settings where disagreements can be aired within earshot of all the parties.

A third bit of advice is not to address issues only when they are intense, become too hardened, or come too late. Should we be for this or that presidential candidate? That is a poor question to ask on the first Monday of November. By the time something has a legislative bill code number on it, it is probably too late to make a contribution to it. It is more important to take up issues that may come to crisis points but represent enduring themes.

Suppose the human race survives; it is hard to picture that the know-how behind the making of nuclear armaments will disappear. There will be weapons. There is no likelihood that the churches will come up with a policy that will remove the weapons and thus clear the congregational agenda. There will instead be constant alterations in the priorities and policies: When ought we talk with the enemy, when must we arm, when do we risk, when can we trust, and which is the best disarmament or armament policy?

Two important steps

Now comes an important step. Various kinds of expertise can be called forth from the congregation or outside resources. Thus the physician, the banker, the lawyer, and the farmer may all have something important to say about an issue from their various perspectives. If they say it in each other's presence, no single profession or no expertise can lord it over others. The moral vision of pastoral leadership, connected with expertise in biblical study, also is essential.

Crucial is the next stage, already implied: Both sides must subject themselves and one another to the Word of God. They have to connect somehow with some norm in the Bible or in the legacy of the church. Thus on the matter of arms, it is legitimate to call on both the tradition of pacifism and the just war, since both of these heritages provide examples of the way Christians have addressed or would address moral issues of war. If these do not satisfy, Christians must find other resources.

One can often attend a discussion on Christian congregational soil and leave three hours later without having heard a single word that differs from what one might hear in a town meeting on television. Older readers will remember Christian debates over open housing. These usually converged on the topics of equity, what happens to property values, and crime, but never on how Christians as believers in God's love in Christ might see the many sides.

A last step

Finally, have each "side" in an issue present some concrete way of addressing the problem. The illustration of the nursing homes again provides an example. While one faction may go to the capitol and the other may go to the nursing home, both go somewhere or provide some kind of support. The process of locating, defining, and addressing issues and drawing upon the Christian tradition finally does not make the church a mere debating society. Somehow it becomes a place where sleeves get rolled up and some action results.

The public place

In these last two chapters we slid very quickly from the private to the political aspects of life. In the process we overlooked a slightly less controversial realm in which one can do good. The political realm is usually seen as one moved mainly by power. A party tries to get 51 percent of the votes for a candidate or a policy. This may be done by crook and by hook, by beguiling propaganda and the buying or trading of votes. At times even good policies come from a corrupt satisfying of interests among lobbying groups.

But it is possible to see public life in other than political terms, even if politics is a part of public life. Christians do well to think of some other theatres of the public, theatres that do not relate at once to the political stump or the polling place.

The public is a place where the company of strangers gather. There they come to know each other and learn why they differ so much from each other. Each group brings its own color, texture, and perhaps even its "smell" of traditions. The Christian moves from that part of public life called church, and bumps into both churched and unchurched people who are motivated by political party, service club, or other interest groups.

The artistic zone

One of the areas of public life that is not directly political is the artistic. The Christian knows that one can "do ill" in the world of arts and entertainment. Pornography, violence, and degradation of the human spirit can be portrayed on gallery walls as well as in magazines and on film. The images then counter the purposes of God. In such expressions bodies are not temples of the Holy Spirit but objects to be used by the powerful and the paying. The virtues that make family life possible are undercut. The beauty of creation is distorted into sensation and ugliness.

Christians cannot fight something with nothing. To complain about "secular humanism" does little good. Christians serve society best by changing their tastes.

Some years ago when a dedicated and militant group of conservative Christians protested a situation comedy on television, the network did some polling. That night, 13.2 percent of the American people were watching this program, *Soap*. What about the people who made up membership in the conservative Christian organization? The survey showed that among those, 13 percent were watching—a mere .2 percent less than the total percentage. Maybe they were all doing their weekly research or satisfying their curiosity about the Devil's ways.

More positively, Christians can do good by helping to create an audience for better programs. When Christians patronize the good films, there can be more good films. Filmmaking is a commercial proposition. Through their colleges and congregational encouragement, Christians can help develop informed audiences for good entertainment and good images on gallery walls.

The marketplace

Another not fully political public zone is the marketplace. Here one can do good by choosing to invest one's self in one way or another. Christians can help run a business in equitable ways or be moved by mere and often unjust selfishness.

The town meeting is another place, for there the "public" is formed. If Christians desert it, they can be spoken about and spoken against, but they cannot be heard.

Each group of Christians can identify more dimensions of "public" in their own communities. Are they to abandon these while they pursue their private faith? Is the new creation not to be evidenced even fragmentarily in the world?

Christian "doing good" in the public realm does not—we cannot say it often enough—reflect all that "being good," being righteous in Christ, is all about. It does not bring people into the reconciling circle of Jesus Christ. But this does not mean that it has nothing to do with the gospel and life under the gospel.

True, people grow curious about the motivations of those who sacrifice for public good. When television or the newspapers tell the story of those motivated by the love of Christ, they sometimes raise suspicions about this love. Unchurched people often interpret the good works of Christians as proud or false displays of goodness or as efforts at "winning" people for church membership. But not all actions for good by Christians in the human city are motivated only by a desire to convert people.

The common good

Christians have much to contribute to the common good. For example, they know the corruption of human nature but need not despair over it. Christians do good in the public realm by helping to avoid foolish utopias that give people false hopes and then disappoint them. They can remind the world that selfishness and other evils are present in human nature. When the secular artist or analyst acknowledges this, there is often a cynical response. But the Christian can draw on a long story and say that God has always been able to use weak human beings for divine purposes.

Furthermore, the Christian who connects a Christ-derived "being good" with human expressions of "doing good" can bring a vision of hope to others who have no hope. This is not mere optimism, which assumes too much about the future's details. The Christian says we do not know enough about the future to be completely pessimistic, and we *do* know enough to know that God will be there, a God who loves and cares. So long as rain falls and the sun shines, that long is God keeping his covenant of care.

Christians at their best

At their best, Christians have contributed institutions and been persons who leave their stamp on the human city. Today most institutions of mercy are not run and paid for by the church, as they once were, but the church does not abandon what it does not entirely fund or administrate. On the basis of several measurements we can say that about half of all voluntarily donated hours and dollars in American public life are gathered and channeled through religious organizations. Most of them are made up of Christians.

Showing mercy to victims of injustice is not the only policy for Christians' doing of good. It is, however, better than not binding wounds at all. Churches that have never spoken for justice can at least develop their claim that works of mercy can compensate in part for injustice. An uninformed society may forget what Christian doctors, nurses, teachers, deacons, deaconnesses, and builders have done in the past, but the story can be made vivid again when their counterparts do these good things in a changed world.

There is always room for the self-starting heroine or hero on Christian soil. These persons, moved by the love of God in Christ, do not calculate whether they can win victories. They need only the cross behind them and the vision of human need before them. They simply witness to the love of God and add credibility to the message of the cross by showing that people moved by it live also in our time.

The need for education

At the same time, most of us are not cast from heroic molds. We have to make provision for passage of Christian moral concern from one generation to the next. This means that the church has to provide agencies—church schools and educational experiences—that pass on the Christian moral vision and the gospel story, which provides the dynamic for Christian moral action.

Childhood education remains urgent. The Sunday church school, the vacation church school, the Christian day school and other forms of weekday education are all historic channels. All are threatened by social change. The family was a nurturing center, but it is unstable. There can be no convergence on a single model of recovery, but there can be instant recognition that unless provision is made, the young will drift.

Attention to late adolescents and young adults is most urgent. In our society, surveys show, people are moved by life-styles. Most who "hang out" with the high-tech, high-living, distracted people make no room for God and make no room for the church. Those in whose lives God and church play a part help turn the way of God into something that is inviting.

Adult education in the church is just beginning to blossom; but it is developing rapidly, and its growth is very promising. As adults become more informed of the basis of their faith and the issues of life, both public and private, that confront them as Christians, they become more equipped to deal with these issues and to witness to others the good life that God wants all to enjoy.

The church cannot raise armies, cannot coerce, cannot tax. It relies on the faith of its members. They get power from shared prayer, shared Bible, shared faith. If they do not renew or refresh themselves at these points, they soon grow sterile and lose motive and power. So the Bible class or adult forum remains a key necessity.

Special opportunities

Christians in America have never pursued the full potential of the lay academy. In this adult education model, members of a single profession meet. The social workers who are Christian converge to test the goals and norms of their work by some Christian criteria. So do the lawyers who work in another realm where so many decisions determine their doing good or doing ill. And the doctors and teachers and homemakers and office or factory workers do the same. Such academies can greatly influence the Christian's public life.

Think of the retreat: Here Christians withdraw from the public world in order to advance again into it. Here the gospel is permitted to touch hearts in a setting away from distraction. Yet few Christians will be content to let this spiritual growth occur away from the real world wherein Christ can be served. Many congregations have found that the retreat can focus well on "Christ and My Job" or "The Ministry of the Christian in the World" and the like.

In conclusion

This study has spent almost no time at all on another use of the term "do good." In our culture an "-ism" has been attached. Do-goodism and do-gooders, especially in the church, meet the disdain of the hard-nosed old or of the suspicious young. Sometimes the charge of do-goodism comes from people who simply want to dismiss from their minds the call to be heroic or sacrificial. Let it also serve as a reminder that "doing good," cut off from its source in "being good," can soon be judgmental and self-centered.

Pastors, teachers, parents, or congregational leaders, then, who want to promote "doing good," not "do-goodism," will have to come, each day, back to base one. That base is at the foot of the cross of Jesus Christ, in sight of an empty tomb. That is the space on the earth where Jesus meets humans, showing them wounds, signaling a glorified body, signing a new creation, and sending his followers on a mission. Such a vision, such a source, will never fail those who let it work its good news on them. That good news produces good ways.